THE
Crafted
Cookie

THE
Crafted Cookie

A Beginner's Guide to Baking & Decorating Cookies for Every Occasion

Anne Yorks

Founder of
The Flour Box

PAGE STREET
PUBLISHING CO.

PAGE STREET
PUBLISHING CO.

First published in 2021 by

Page Street Publishing Co.

27 Congress Street, Suite 105

Salem, MA 01970

www.pagestreetpublishing.com

Distributed by Macmillan, sales in Canada by The Canadian Manda Group.

25 24 23 22 21   1 2 3 4 5

ISBN-13: 978-1-64567-225-8

ISBN-10: 1-64567-225-5

Library of Congress Control Number: 2020945235

Cover and book design by Rosie Stewart for Page Street Publishing Co.

Photography by Elise Cellucci

Printed and bound in the United States

Page Street Publishing protects our planet by donating to nonprofits like The Trustees, which focuses on local land conservation.

Dedication

Table of Contents

Introduction

Get ready for amazing cookie adventures!

The cookie world is a place where your creativity is made delicious! I'm Anne Yorks, a cookie artist, and I'm excited to share this book with you—filled with my recipes and tons of cookie inspiration to make your celebrations just a little sweeter. Let's have some fun!

FIND THE JOY IN DECORATING, NOT THE STRESS

Before you get started, let me tell you that *you can do this*! Maybe you've watched a few cookie videos or have seen pretty cookies in a magazine and thought to yourself, "I could never do that." Trust me. You can! With a little planning, lots of sugar and this book, you'll be whipping up batches of treats that will make your loved ones smile.

Just have fun decorating and don't worry too much about things being perfect. These tutorials will take you through each project step-by-step. While you decorate, just remind yourself that someone is going eat this art . . . and love it. Yum! Go ahead and make a few mistakes—and then gobble them up!

COOKIE DECORATING IS A LABOR OF LOVE

But it is so worth it! Use my lists to help you prep. Try to break up the process over the span of a couple of days to fit it into a busy schedule. I suggest some tips on planning a cookie timeline on page 24. I share how I navigate the cookie process and plan for success. Also, I hope you love my work space overview on pages 26 to 27.

WORKING WITH ROYAL ICING

The cookies in this book are decorated with a simple, straightforward royal icing—a delicious icing that dries hard, like a candy. Royal icing is ideal for cookie decorating and making party favors because, once the icing dries, you can stack and pack these cookies without worrying about the package materials sticking to the icing.

The first pages of this book feature my yummy cookie and icing recipes that have delighted cookie lovers since 2007. The next several pages are an amazing resource dedicated to helping cookie decorating newbies understand royal icing: how to make it, store it and use it. Using my icing consistency guide on page 16 is key when it comes to successful decorating!

Working with royal icing takes practice, but don't give up. Once you get the hang of it, the results are magnificent!

CREATING THE PERFECT COOKIE PLATTER

Cookies are in season all year round! In this book, you'll find inspiration for life's big events and each season of the year. I planned each cookie set to maximize not only your time, but also your creativity.

Each platter has one *feature cookie*. This cookie is the most beautiful to look at from the set. It has multiple icing areas, fun techniques and a few extra details. It will take longer to make these cookies, but they are each the star of the platter!

Each cookie set will also include two (or sometimes three) *accent cookies*. These cookies are simpler in design, requiring fewer steps to make, but are still tons of fun to create. Working accent cookies into the platter helps reduce your decorating time. Plus, sometimes guests are intimidated to eat a feature cookie, but they will always grab and gobble up an accent cookie. I love creating cookie platters that have something for both the eyes and the stomach!

THE PLANNING IS DONE, SO JUST HAVE SOME FUN

Each of the fifteen cookie platters in the book includes a cookie yield, so you can plan how many cookies to make. I also share an icing plan for each set. Check out my estimates of how much of each color to make and their consistencies. The tool list will help you get ready to decorate. Each set is broken down by cookie with step-by-step directions. Use the photos and written instructions to re-create each cookie. Or feel free to use my example as a jumping off point to get creative.

COOKIE CONFIDENCE

No more delays, it's time to jump in and get started. Like any new craft, you'll have cookie decorating trials and errors. But, practice *bakes* perfect! Remember to share all your creations with others—this art is made to be eaten. I can't wait for you to experience the joy of giving the gift of hand-decorated cookies!

Happy decorating!

Cookie Decorating 101

The following pages break down the cookie-decorating process and include the essentials you need to know to get started. I tried to answer all the questions I had when I first started decorating cookies. I share my cookie and icing recipes, a review of icing consistencies, coloring tips, suggestions for how to store cookies and icing, tips for setting up a cookie plan and an overview of basic decorating techniques.

I don't want you to be overwhelmed. This information is here not only to answer your questions as you get started, but also to serve as a reference that you can come back to as you move through your cookie adventures.

Foolproof Cut-Out Cookie Recipe

This delicious cut-out cookie recipe bakes to a golden color and has a buttery, vanilla flavor. The texture is soft, yet still has a bit of a crunch. This recipe can be doubled in most 5-quart (4.7-L) or larger stand mixers.

Yield: *18 to 24 cookies (varies on size and thickness)*

Active Time: *30 minutes for mixing the dough + 60 minutes for rolling and baking*

Inactive Time: *2 hours to chill the dough*

- 1 cup (2 sticks [227 g]) butter, softened
- 1 cup (200 g) granulated white sugar
- 1 large egg
- 1½ tsp (7 ml) Butter Vanilla Bakery Emulsion flavoring
- ½ tsp salt (omit if using salted butter)
- 2¾ cups (343 g) all-purpose flour, plus a little extra for rolling

MIXING THE DOUGH

Step 1: Using a stand mixer fitted with the paddle attachment, or a large bowl and a hand mixer, cream together the softened butter and sugar until light and fluffy.

Step 2: Add the egg and vanilla flavoring and mix to incorporate. I like to use emulsions because the flavor does not bake out. Butter vanilla is delicious! Substitute your favorite bakery emulsion flavor or extract— pure vanilla, lemon, almond—teaspoon for teaspoon.

Step 3: Add ½ teaspoon of salt if using unsalted butter. Add the flour 1 cup (125 g) at a time. Make sure to fluff the flour then spoon it into your measuring cup (don't scoop it), then scrape extra off the top. Use precise measurements and avoid adding too much flour to your recipe. Mix on low just until incorporated. Overmixing can result in a tougher cookie. The dough will form a ball and come away from the sides of the mixer.

TIP:

If the dough is crumbling and looks dry, you've added too much flour. You can fix your dough by adding more liquid (water or milk). Add 1 teaspoon at a time to get to the desired texture. This small amount of liquid will not affect the taste of the dough.

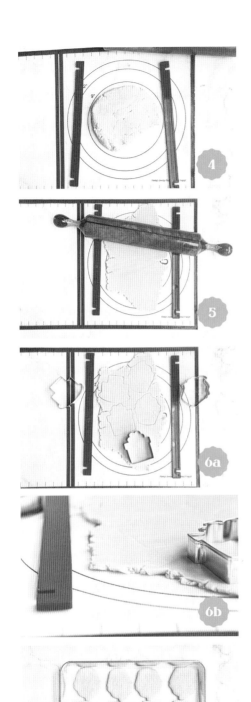

Step 4: Scrape the dough from the bowl and put it on plastic wrap. Flatten the dough to a disc shape to make it easier to roll after chilling. Wrap it well, making sure all the edges of dough are covered. Chill the dough for at least 2 hours before rolling out.

ROLLING OUT THE COOKIES

Step 5: On a pastry mat or a lightly floured surface, use a floured rolling pin to roll out the dough. Roll cookies to ¼-inch (6-mm) thickness. Use pastry sticks or rolling pin bands to get an even thickness.

Step 6: Use cookie cutters to cut out the cookies. Place the cut-outs on cookie sheets lined with parchment paper. Parchment paper prevents the cookies from sticking to the sheet and also makes for even browning.

Step 7: Collect the dough scraps into a ball, re-roll and cut more cookies to use the full batch of dough.

BAKING THE COOKIES

Step 8: Preheat the oven to 350°F (176°C).

Step 9: Bake for 11 to 13 minutes. Watch them carefully at the end. When done, the cookies should be light golden brown on the edges.

Step 10: Cool the cookies completely before decorating, about 1 hour. It's important to cool them completely or the royal icing will melt off! If needed, you can pop the freshly baked cookies in the fridge or freezer for a few minutes to cool faster.

Royal Icing Recipe

Royal icing is ideal for cookie decorating. It dries hard like a candy, allowing decorators to make interesting textures and add dimension to the designs. And, once the icing is dry, the cookies can be stacked on a platter or packed in a cute treat bag without worrying about sticky icing! The key ingredient in royal icing is the meringue powder, a food-safe alternative to using raw egg whites. You can find meringue powder online and in craft stores in the baking aisle.

Yield: *18 to 20 oz (530 to 600 ml) of icing*

Active Time: *15 minutes to mix icing + 45 minutes to make colors and bag icing*

Inactive Time: *None*

- ⅓ cup (80 ml) warm water, plus more to adjust icing consistencies
- 1 tsp vanilla (I use imitation clear vanilla, but pure vanilla extract works great, too)
- ¼ cup (36 g) meringue powder
- 1 lb (4 cups [454 g]) powdered sugar
- 2 tsp (10 ml) white gel food coloring (optional)

MIXING THE ICING

Step 1: Pour the warm water into the bowl of a stand mixer arranged with the paddle attachment, or into a large mixing bowl if using a hand mixer. Add the vanilla and meringue powder. Mix for a minute on medium speed until fluffy and foamy. Scrape the sides of the bowl if necessary.

Step 2: Once the water and meringue powder mixture is fluffy and foamy, add the powdered sugar in stages. Keep the mixer on low, adding sugar slowly to avoid a powdery explosion. I find it is not necessary to sift powdered sugar, but you may do so if you prefer.

Step 3: Once all the sugar is added, increase the speed to 4 (or a medium-low speed). The amount of mixing time can vary from 4 to 7 minutes depending on the humidity. Beat the icing until it changes from ivory to a brighter white. After a few minutes of mixing, you'll notice the icing will form stiff peaks and will increase in size. It will go from looking pasty to smooth. Take care not to overmix, though. If the icing looks spongy and fluffy like marshmallow, it will not perform!

TIP:

You can adjust your icing consistencies. If your icing seems too stiff, add another tablespoon or two (15 to 30 ml) of water to loosen the icing a bit. I like to mix the icing thick, and then use water to bring it to a nice soft-peak/piping icing consistency. If your icing appears too thin, and stiff peaks are not forming, add more sugar, ¼ cup (30 g) at a time, to make the icing thicker. See the next page for more details on adjusting icing consistencies.

Step 4 (optional): Add 2 teaspoons (10 ml) of white food color to the icing if you'd like a beautiful pure and bright white icing. This will also allow your other icing colors to pop even more.

Step 5: Separate the icing into small containers (one for each color you'll need) and seal with an airtight lid until ready to mix the icing colors. Do not leave the icing without an airtight cover or it will form a crust. Note that I usually adjust the consistency to piping icing (see next page) and then store it. If the project requires stiff icing (like the pink icing for the birthday set on page 31), I'll take out the stiff icing that is needed first before adjusting the rest of the batch to piping consistency. It's just easier to let the mixer do the mixing.

Piping icing

Royal Icing Consistencies

An understanding of icing consistencies is essential to successful cookie decorating. It is more important to get the right icing consistencies than it is to follow the Royal Icing Recipe exactly. If your icing seems too thin, add a bit of powdered sugar to thicken the consistency. If it seems too thick, add a few drops of water. Making these tweaks before you bag your icing will make a big difference in the final results.

COMMON ICING CONSISTENCIES

I love to outline with a piping icing and then flood the cookies with a thinner flood icing. I have found you can get the best results when using two icing consistencies.

Piping icing (a.k.a. soft-peak icing): This icing is used for piping outlines and piping most cookie details. I compare the consistency of piping icing to a soft-serve ice cream. When you dip your spatula into the icing and pull it out, the icing will hold its shape, but still have a little motion. I like to look for the swirl to know I have it just right. For 8 ounces (237 ml) of icing, I typically add 1 teaspoon of water to get to soft-peak consistency. You might need to make adjustments: If the icing is too thick, start by adding ½ teaspoon of water (or several drops) at a time. If the icing is too runny, add 1 tablespoon (8 g) of powdered sugar. Small tweaks will help you zero in on the right consistency.

Flood icing

Flood icing (a.k.a. 10-second icing): This is the icing that flows onto the surface of the cookie to create a flat canvas. This icing is thinner than the piping icing because it has more water. I compare the consistency of flood icing to fresh honey. For 8 ounces (237 ml) of icing, I typically add 2 to 3 teaspoons (10 to 15 ml) of water to piping icing to get it to the flood consistency. It has slow flow, but is not runny or watery. To test if your icing is at the right consistency, use the edge of a spatula to draw a line in the icing. It should take 10 seconds for the line to disappear in the icing.

If the icing is too thin, you'll see many air bubbles (in the bowl and/or on the flooded cookie surface). Eliminate the bubble issue by making the icing at the 10-second consistency. Make adjustments as needed (as with piping icing—adding small amounts of water or powdered sugar to make the icing thinner or thicker). See how to adjust icing in action in the royal icing video on my YouTube channel @theflourboxshop! On YouTube simply search "Flour Box Royal Icing" to find the video.

Thick icing

Medium icing

I don't use these icing consistencies on every project, but use them occasionally for specific decorating reasons.

Thick icing (a.k.a. stiff-peak icing): This icing is used for stenciling, icing flowers or shell borders. I compare this icing to a meringue. When you dip your spatula into the icing and pull it out, the icing will hold its shape and form a stiff peak. There is no motion. This is the consistency of the icing straight out of the mixer. No water is added to adjust to this consistency.

Medium icing (a.k.a. 20-second icing): This is a medium icing consistency in between piping and flooding icing, used to decorate small areas or mini cookies. I compare this icing consistency to yogurt: not flowing, but eventually self-leveling. It should be thin enough to have a bit of flow, but thick enough to hold its shape. With this icing, you can pipe and flood all from the same bag. For 8 ounces (237 ml) of icing, I typically add 1 to 2 teaspoons (5 to 10 ml) of water to piping icing.

A great example of 20-second icing is the stick on the popsicle on page 113. It is easier to make this "middle-of-the-road" icing so that the small area can be piped and flooded with one bag. You can test this icing in the same way as the 10-second icing. Draw a line through it with your spatula and count how long it takes for the line to disappear—it should be about 20 seconds.

Coloring Icing and Building Piping Bags

Step 1: To start coloring the icing, put drops of food color on a spatula, as opposed to squeezing the color directly into the bowl. This will prevent too much color from being added to the icing. Then stir the color into the icing, taking care to incorporate it completely to get a solid tone throughout.

I recommend food gels for coloring icing. I like the Chefmaster brand, but there are several good gel options. You can find them online or at a craft store in the baking aisle. Food coloring gels are different than what you find at the grocery store—they aren't watery and won't change the consistency of the icing when you add color. Gels are also concentrated and typically less color is needed as a result. For deep colors, like red, black and navy, often ¼ teaspoon of gel will be needed to color 8 ounces (237 ml) of icing. For medium tones, I use three to five drops of color on average to color 8 ounces (237 ml) of icing. When making pastel icing colors, usually one to three drops is sufficient for 8 ounces (237 ml) of icing. These amounts are proportionate and will vary based on the amount of icing you're coloring.

PREP THE ICING BAGS:

Step 2: To build a piping bag, you'll need a bag, a coupler and an icing tip. Insert the large piece of the coupler inside the piping bag. Trim off the opening.

Step 3: Put the icing tip on the bag.

Step 4: Screw on the second piece of the coupler to hold the tip in place. When you'd like to switch tips, simply unscrew this second piece, remove the tip, load your new tip and screw the coupler piece back on!

I use a glass to hold my icing bag while I fill it. Wrap the icing bag over the edge of the glass. A damp paper towel in the bottom of the glass helps keep the tips from drying out.

FILLING THE ICING BAGS

Do the following steps for each icing color:

Step 5: Remove a small portion of colored icing (approximately 1 ounce [30 ml]) for piping and put it in an icing bag fitted with the coupler and tip. (See page 16 for details on achieving the ideal piping icing consistency.) Add a twist tie or bag band to the end of the bag to prevent any icing from squeezing up and out of the bag while decorating.

Step 6: Then use the remaining colored icing in the container for flood icing. Add a small amount of water—about 2 or 3 teaspoons (10 to 15 ml) of water per 8 ounces (237 ml) of icing—to thin it down to the flood icing consistency. Do the 10-second test with your spatula to double-check that it is not too thin or thick (see page 16 for details on making flood icing). It helps to add the water 1 teaspoon at a time; when you are close to the right consistency but not quite there yet, add just one or two drops at a time.

Step 7: Pour the flood icing into a disposable icing bag. Less control is needed for the flooding icing and I generally do not use a tip on flood icing bags. Eliminating the tips makes cleaning up easy—just throw away the bag when finished.

Step 8: Trim the bag just before decorating. To get a round opening, hold the tipless bag so that the seam is pointing up, then snip a tiny opening. You can always make it bigger if needed, but start small so you have control over the flow of icing.

Storing and Planning Royal Icing

STORE YOUR ROYAL ICING

Mix the icing the day before decorating to allow the colors to fully develop. This will also break up the decorating process.

First, make your icing. Then separate it into bowls to make the colors. Add the food gel and color each icing. Cover each bowl with a lid to prevent a crust from forming. I store icing overnight in airtight containers at piping consistency. I do not adjust the different icing consistencies until the next day, just before I decorate. Piping icing doesn't have the tendency to separate, but if you make *flood* icing the day before you decorate, you'll notice this thinner icing will separate. The fluff will rise to the top, and the water and heavier sugars sink to the bottom of the bowl. You can stir and remix if this happens, but generally I avoid this issue by mixing my flood right before jumping into the actual decorating.

The next day, just before decorating, adjust the icing consistencies (usually piping and flood) and bag the icing.

When using meringue powder, store icing on a countertop for up to 2 days. If using a Royal Icing Recipe with egg whites, store the icing in the refrigerator.

If working a few *days* in advance, store icing in the refrigerator for up to a week. If working a few *weeks* in advance (like for a big cookie project), store icing in the freezer in a freezer-quality air-tight container. If packed well, icing can be stored this way for up to 3 months. Thaw the icing for a few hours before decorating.

HOW MUCH SHOULD I MAKE?

A single batch of dough will yield 18 to 24 cookies. This will vary based on the size and thickness of the cookies. When making a single batch of dough, plan to make a single batch of royal icing (18 to 20 ounces [530 to 600 ml]).

The cookie recipe can be doubled in a stand mixer. A double batch of dough will make 36 to 48 cookies. For a double batch of dough, plan to make a double batch of royal icing (36 to 40 ounces [1.1 to 1.2 L])

PLANNING ICING COLORS

Write a plan for making icing colors. For one average-size cookie, about 3.5 inches (9 cm) in diameter, plan 1 ounce (30 ml) of icing. Each set in this cookie book already has a suggested color plan! However, you can use the chart on the next page to help you plan your own cookies, or if you'd like to change the colors from what I've suggested.

Total Number of Cookies: _____

Dough Needed: _____

Icing Needed: _____

ICING COLOR CHART

ICING COLOR	SIZE AND NUMBER OF COOKIES	OUNCES OF ICING	PIPE	FLOOD	STIFF OR 20S

Common Cookie Decorating Techniques

Outlining

Flooding

Throughout the instructions of the book, I'll be using several common terms to describe the cookie decorating techniques. Here is an overview.

PIPING

This is the action of squeezing out thicker icing for outlines and details. I'm right-handed, so I hold the icing bag in the palm of my right hand to have control over my hand pressure (how hard I'm squeezing the bag). I keep the pointer finger of my left hand on the coupler to balance or steady myself while piping lines. You can reverse hands if your left hand is dominant.

OUTLINING

Adding a border or outline to the cookie creates a wall or barrier for the thin flood icing to rest against, so it doesn't spill over the edge of the cookie. When I pipe outlines, I don't drag the tip across the surface of the cookie, but rather lift it up and off while squeezing and allow the icing fall onto the cookie. This will keep the outline round and raised up to hold back the flood.

If you made a mistake, use the flat end of a boo-boo stick (see #7 in the photo of my workspace on pages 26 to 27) to scrape off the icing, then repipe that section.

PIPED ACCENTS AND TECHNIQUES

Piping straight lines, wavy lines, loops, vines, scrolls, hearts and dots on cookies is a common way to add decorative accents. I share tips for these piping techniques on the tutorial pages, but practicing these basics is helpful in making beautiful cookies. See the piping practice sheet on page 146. Copy this page and use up leftover icing to practice these over and over. You'll be amazed at how quickly your lines will steady. You can watch me pipe the practice sheet and demonstrate these accents on the video tutorial on our YouTube channel @theflourboxshop. On YouTube simply search "Flour Box Practice Sheet."

FLOODING IN THE COOKIE

This is the action of filling in the base icing layer of the cookie. Squeeze the 10-second icing onto the cookie surface and watch it self-level, creating a beautiful, flat surface when dry.

Again, I keep the icing bag firmly in the palm of my right hand. I use the pointer finger on my left hand near the base of the bag to steady myself. (Do the reverse if your left hand is dominant.)

I like to flood the cookie generously to have a beautiful finish to the icing. I first bump the flood icing against the outline to create a seamless look for the edge of the whole area I am flooding. Then I flood the area in completely, not leaving any of the cookie showing. If you don't add enough, when the icing dries the base layer won't be flat and the icing will look lumpy or have "hills and valleys."

Tap the icing into place using the scribe tool (or a toothpick). Pop any air bubbles with the tip of a scribe tool or a toothpick.

WET-ON-WET TECHNIQUES

This is a term that refers to icing patterns created with the flood icing (not the piping icing) while the flood icing is still wet. Typically, the base layer of the icing is flooded in, then a second color is added to create a wet-on-wet pattern. The two icing colors melt together and create a flat surface.

Wet-on-Wet Polka Dots

It's important that the icing consistencies match because otherwise the flood might not achieve a flat surface. If the accent icing color is too thick, it will be raised and won't melt to create the flat layer. If the icing is too thin, it will spread out and not hold its shape, or may even crack.

The two steps of the wet-on-wet technique, flooding and adding the accent color, are done back to back while the icing is still wet. If too much time passes, the base icing will set up and the added color will not melt into the background to create a flat surface. Take into account that you'll be adding more icing with the second color. To prevent an overflow, be careful not to add too much icing to the base layer.

Polka dots: This is the most common wet-on-wet technique. Drops of flood icing are added to the base icing as polka dots to create a cute or whimsical background. See the Dottie Spring Chicken on page 86 for an example of this technique.

Stripes: Wet-on-wet stripes are another common "background" pattern. The key to creating wet-on-wet stripes is trimming a very small opening on the flood bag to maximize control over the icing flow or the width of the stripe. See the Snuggly Body Suit on page 43 for an example of wet-on-wet stripes.

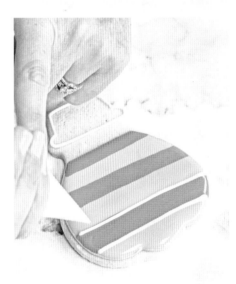

Wet-on-Wet Stripes

Marbling: This wet-on-wet technique looks intricate and difficult, but I assure you it's lots of fun and very easy. This technique builds off of the wet-on-wet stripes. I like to use at least two icing colors when marbling, but it can be more. Once stripes are added, a scribe (or toothpick) is dragged through the icing to create the marbled look. See the Up, Up and Away Hot Air Balloon on page 78 for an example of marbling.

Get creative with wet-on-wet techniques! Once you get the hang of them, you can really start to have fun. The clouds on the Sweet Dreams Footie Pajama (page 38) and the mini daisies on the Blooming Rubber Boot (page 94) are both examples of a more custom wet-on-wet design.

The Cookie Process

Before you start a project, it is helpful to plan a cookie timeline, especially if you're working around a busy home or work schedule. Not only do you need to plan for each phase—the prep, baking, decorating and packing—but it is important to understand that royal icing takes time to fully dry before packing cookies.

I like to break up the decorating process as follows below. It fits better in my life than tackling everything in one day. The following times are based on a single batch of cookies; adjust as needed. They are also based on my average speed, but if you're a complete cookie beginner, expect that you might take a bit longer as you figure things out. Help yourself and set up your own personal plan by timing how long it takes you to do each phase. Then you'll have a better reference for your decorating speed for planning future cookie projects.

DAY 1: PREP COOKIES AND ICING
- Mix the dough (30 minutes)
- Chill the dough (2 hours inactive time)
- Roll and bake the cookies (1 hour)
- Mix the royal icing and prep the icing colors (1 hour)

DAY 2: DECORATE
- Outllne and flood the cookies (1 to 2 hours)
- Allow the cookies to dry in front of a fan before adding details (30 minutes to 2 hours inactive time for standard cookies, but allow 6 hours of dry time if stenciling on the surface of the cookie)
- Add details, including detail piping, airbrushing and stenciling (1 to 2 hours)

DAY 3: PACK COOKIES
** Allow cookies to fully dry for 18 to 24 hours before packaging. Store in a cool oven overnight. **
- Put the cookies in a treat bag and add a ribbon (45 minutes)

TIPS FOR PACKAGING, WRAPPING AND SHIPPING COOKIES

Individually wrapping cookies: Find treat bags in the food crafting aisle at most big box craft stores. Use the 4 x 8–inch (10 x 20–cm) bags if adding a ribbon. Be sure to allow the icing to fully dry (18 to 24 hours) before packaging cookies to prevent the icing from sticking to the bag.

Boxing cookies: Use a window bakery box to present cookies. I like 14-inch (35-cm) boxes like those from BRP Box Shop for 1 to 2 dozen cookies.

Shipping cookies: Wrap cookies individually and then slip them into a bubble pouch. Pack the bubble-wrapped cookies into a bakery box with crinkle paper as a cushion between the cookies. Then put that box in a shipping box. I fill in the space with packing peanuts. Do a jiggle test. There shouldn't be any movement. If you do feel movement, add more crinkle or peanuts to make sure everything is fully cushioned. I like to double-box the cookies like this to prevent them from breaking.

Once the cookies are packed, I suggest they be eaten within 2 weeks. I prefer to store cookies in a treat bag with a twist tie for maximum freshness (and a nice presentation), but you can also store them in an airtight container. Put a piece of parchment or wax paper between cookie layers to prevent butter marks from cookies resting on each other.

I have frozen both decorated and undecorated cookies with success. This helps me plan baking and decorating when I can fit it into my schedule, and not feel like I must complete every project the day before a celebration. I use a freezer-quality bag or container and keep my freezer free of any funky smells (Arm & Hammer baking soda is helpful).

When freezing undecorated cookies, stack them up on each other, usually six per stack, with four stacks fitting nicely in a freezer bag. When you are ready to decorate, take the cookies out of the freezer and allow them to come to room temperature before decorating.

When freezing decorated cookies, allow 18 hours of dry time for the icing before packing and freezing. Wrap cookies individually and then put them in the freezer bag. When you're ready to take them out, allow the cookies to come to room temperature before opening the bag. This prevents condensation from forming in the bag and causing any icing issues. If you're uncertain about freezing cookies, do a taste test. I bet you can't tell the difference!

Time-Saving Tips

Be a smart cookie—here are a few tips to save time while decorating cookies!

GET THE ASSEMBLY LINE GOING

Create an assembly line for your cookie decorating. In other words, I like to group tasks. Not only does the repetition of doing the same task speed things up, but it will also make your cookies look more consistent. First, I outline all of the cookies. Then, I start flooding in the cookies. After that, I add the details. I work tray by tray. As the decorating time passes, the icing I did at the beginning is setting up. Usually when I get back to the first tray, the icing is completely set up and I'm ready to move to the next step. Tackling the full process cookie by cookie isn't wrong, but it can mean you'll be picking up and putting down your tools a lot, which will really tack on the time while decorating.

Generally, I like to start decorating with the feature cookies—or the cookies that will have the most steps to complete. While they are drying, I work on the easier accent cookies.

DECORATE ON THE TRAY

I prefer to decorate directly on a cookie sheet (see the cookie sheet photo from my work space on the next two pages). I just jump from cookie to cookie as I move down the line. Usually three rows of four average-size cookies will fit on a cookie sheet. I am most comfortable when I'm decorating close to me; it feels awkward to stretch my arms too far when piping details. As a result, I will decorate the middle row first, then the row closest to me. I'll flip the cookie sheet upside-down and complete the final row. No need to set up a special mat or space for the decorating—moving your cookies back and forth takes time. Plus, you won't have to worry about accidentally sticking your finger into freshly piped details!

1. Cookie sheet with parchment paper (see page 25 for tips on using a cookie sheet for assembly-line decorating!)

2. Piping bags

3. Coupler

4. Icing tip for piping icing

5. Glass with damp paper towel to prevent tips from drying out

6. Scribe (or toothpick)

7. Boo-boo stick

8. Food-safe brushes

9. Paper towel

10. Cookie cutters

11. Small mixing dish to hold dusts and sprinkles

12. Sprinkles!

13. Gold dust

14. Carnation pink dust

15. Diamondust edible glitter

16. Food-safe marker

17. Templates (see page 145)

18. Scissors

19. Bag ties

20. Stencils

21. Stencil Genie

22. Scraper

23. Sprayable food color (an alternative to using an airbrush machine)

My Work Space for Decorating Cookies

Celebrate
WITH
Cookies

No matter the celebration, cookies can play a sweet role in life's big moments. They are personal, packable and colorful. Cookies can be the highlight of a dessert table or an impressive and elegant party favor.

In this chapter, enjoy learning how to decorate a colorful Rainbow Birthday set (page 31) that has sweet sprinkle accents. Then dive into the dreamy Twinkle, Twinkle Little Star Baby Shower collection (page 37). After that, get inspired to make wedding cookies with ruffles and flowers (page 45), perfect for a bridal shower or the big day.

Rainbow Birthday

Decorated cookies make a special birthday celebration even sweeter. This Rainbow Birthday cookie set is over the top with vibrant neon colors and fun sprinkle accents. The feature cookie of this platter is the birthday cake. The accent cookies are the cupcake and the present with bow. You can make these cookies as a set or just pick one design to keep things simple. Just keep in mind that the feature birthday cake cookie has more steps and is the most time-consuming to create.

Yield: *18 cookies total (6 birthday cakes, 6 cupcakes and 6 presents)*

TO MAKE THIS PLATTER YOU'LL NEED

- 1 batch Foolproof Cut-Out Cookie dough (page 12)
- 1 batch Royal Icing (page 14)
- Icing colors (I used Chefmaster, see "Colors by the Ounce")

CUTTERS

- Birthday Cake with Candles cookie cutter
- Cupcake with Swirl cookie cutter
- Present with Bow cookie cutter

TIPS AND TOOLS

- 7 tips #2
- 1 Wilton tip #13
- 1 Ateco tip #44
- 7 couplers
- 11 icing bags (7 icing bags for piping and 4 bags, or bottles, for flooding)
- Parchment paper
- Cookie sheets
- Toothpick or scribe
- Rainbow nonpareils
- Coffee filter or paper towel (optional)

STEP 1: PREP THE COOKIES

Use the Foolproof Cut-Out Cookie Recipe on page 12 to bake your cookies, cutting six of each cookie cutter design.

STEP 2: MIX THE ICING AND PREP THE COLORS

Use the Royal Icing Recipe on page 14 to mix a single batch of icing (18 to 20 ounces [530 to 600 ml]). Divide the icing into bowls and make the seven icing colors according to the guide below (refer to page 18 for tips).

STEP 3: ADJUST THE ICING CONSISTENCY

When you're ready to decorate, adjust the consistency of the different icing colors to create piping icing and flooding icing (including the stiff piping icing for the pink) according to the amounts below. For a refresher on making icing consistencies, see page 16. Once the icing colors and consistencies are ready, prep them into piping bags, referring to the individual decorating tutorials for details.

COLORS BY THE OUNCE

- White Icing: 6 oz (180 ml) (1 oz [30 ml] for pipe and 5 oz [150 ml] for flood)
- Neon Pink Icing: 5 oz (150 ml) (1 oz [30 ml] for *stiff* pipe and 4 oz [120 ml] for flood)
- Neon Blue Icing: 3 oz (90 ml) (1 oz [30 ml] for pipe and 2 oz [60 ml] for flood)
- Neon Yellow Icing: 2 oz (60 ml) (1 oz [30 ml] for pipe and 1 oz [30 ml] for flood)
- Neon Orange Icing: 1 oz (30 ml) (for pipe only)
- Neon Green Icing: 1 oz (30 ml) (for pipe only)
- Neon Purple Icing: 1 oz (30 ml) (for pipe only)

Now that your cookies and icing are prepped, it's time to decorate! Use the instructions for each individual cookie to help decorate this Rainbow Birthday cookie platter!

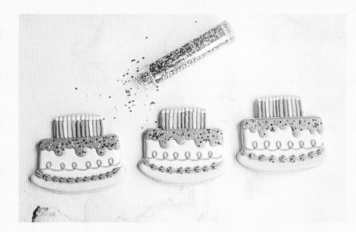

Rainbow Cake with Candles Cookie

This cake is not only dripping with icing, it's dripping with lots of fun rainbow details! Don't forget to add some whimsical icing loops and a delicious shell border. Plus, you can customize the number of candles and add a birthday message to make this cookie extra special!

Yield: *6 cookies*

OUTLINE THE COOKIES

Step 1: Start with piping the dripping icing first. Using pink piping icing and a tip #2, pipe a line across the top of the cake. Then add the drips by wiggling and squiggling across the cake. There is no wrong way to do this. Just have fun! Outline the main body of the cake next using white piping icing and a tip #2. Finally, add the platter using yellow piping icing and a tip #2.

FLOOD THE COOKIES

Step 2: Fill the main section of the cake first using white flood icing.

Stop and dry the iced cookies in front of a fan for 1 hour before flooding the next sections. It's helpful to work in groups of cookies. While one tray is drying, move onto the next tray. See my notes on decorating in an assembly line on page 25.

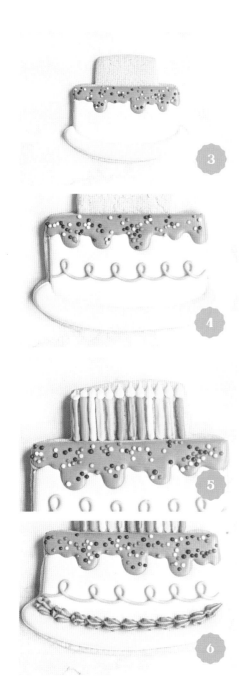

Step 3: Flood the dripping icing using the pink flood. Bump the flood over the pink outlines to bring it to the foreground and give the illusion that it is dripping down over the cake. While the pink icing is still wet, shake on the rainbow nonpareils. You can place the cookie on a coffee filter (or paper towel) before adding the sprinkles to catch any that don't stick. Funnel extras back into the sprinkle container and reuse.

Fill in the platter section with yellow flood icing.

Stop and dry the iced cookies in front of a fan for 30 minutes before adding the details.

ADD THE DETAILS

Step 4: Add icing loops using neon blue piping icing and a tip #2. Use an even medium-pressure hand squeeze and allow the piping tip to guide the shape of the loops, dropping onto the surface of the icing. Six loops fit well in this space.

Step 5: Add the candles using all the neon rainbow colors in piping icing and a tip #2. I added twelve candles, two of each color, but you can customize the number for the guest of honor. Add the flame by squeezing a teardrop shape of yellow piping icing with a tip #2 on the top of each candle.

Step 6: Finish the cookie with a shell border at the base of the cake. Use the pink piping icing with the star tip #13 and pipe a teardrop or shell shape. It is helpful if this piping icing is stiff so that the shell holds its shape. Overlap the next teardrop onto the tail of the previous one. Continue to complete the continuous line across the bottom of the cake.

Sprinkles Galore Cupcake Cookie

Would you like rainbow sprinkles on your cupcake? Yes please, with a cherry on top! This classic birthday treat is totally adorable in cookie form!

Yield: *6 cookies*

OUTLINE THE COOKIES

Step 1: Outline the cherry first by piping a small circle using pink piping icing and a tip #2, then outline the frosting using white piping icing and a tip #2. Start with the bottom layer and work your way up, creating three icing areas. Pipe the cupcake wrapper using blue piping icing and a tip #2.

FLOOD THE COOKIES

Step 2: Flood the wrapper with blue flood icing, then fill the second layer of frosting with white flood icing. Fill the cherry with pink flood icing. While the pink icing is still wet, add a teardrop shape with white flood icing (this wet-on-wet technique allows the highlight to be flat).

Stop and dry the iced cookies in front of a fan for 1 hour before flooding the next sections.

Step 3: Flood the remaining layers of frosting using the white flood icing.

Stop and dry the iced cookies in front of a fan for 30 minutes before adding the details.

ADD THE DETAILS

Step 4: Pipe lines on the cupcake wrapper using blue piping icing and a tip #2. Use the six neon rainbow colors and pipe short lines for the sprinkles. Add them in all directions to look like real sprinkles. I like piping these because the icing colors match the other cookies and I like to have the control over the sprinkle placement, but feel free to use real sprinkles if you prefer. They would need to be added just after flooding these areas so the sprinkles stick to the icing.

All Wrapped Up Birthday Present Cookie

It's not a birthday unless there are presents, and this cheerful cookie with a rainbow sprinkle bow is sure to be a sweet gift!

Yield: *6 cookies*

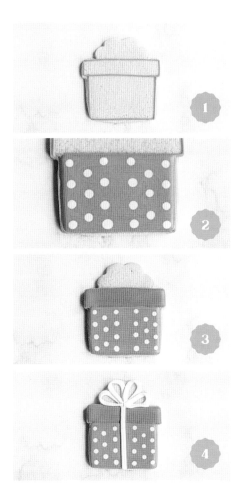

OUTLINE THE COOKIES

Step 1: Outline the lid of the present with pink piping icing and a tip #2. Outline the box with pink piping icing and a tip #2.

FLOOD THE COOKIES

Step 2: Create an interesting pattern on this cookie with wet-on-wet polka dots. Only use flood icing for this technique. First, flood the main section of the present using pink flood icing. While the pink base is still very wet, add drops of white flood icing to create the polka dot pattern. Take care not to dip your tip into the base icing. Just let the drop of icing fall onto the surface and it will melt into the pink, creating a flat surface.

Stop and dry the iced cookies in front of a fan for 1 hour before flooding the next section.

Step 3: Fill in the top of the box with pink flood icing.

Stop and dry the iced cookies in front of a fan for 30 minutes before adding the details.

ADD THE DETAILS

Step 4: Add the ribbon with white piping icing and the tip #44. Start with the straight line in the middle of the box. Keep the tip flat while piping. Then, still keeping the tip flat, pipe four loops for the ribbon on the top of the gift. While the icing is still wet, place the cookie on a coffee filter or paper towel and sprinkle on the rainbow nonpareils (see the final photo at the top of the page for how it looks with the sprinkles).

Twinkle, Twinkle Little Star Baby Shower

Dreaming of the perfect cookie set for a baby shower? Celebrating the arrival of a new bundle of joy? This Twinkle, Twinkle Little Star–themed collection will send the parents-to-be over the moon! Plus, if you make one less of each cookie, you could add in some simple cloud cookies (page 81)! The feature cookie of this platter is the footie pajama. The accent cookies are the star, body suit and baby carriage. You can make these cookies as a set or just pick one design to keep things simple. Tweak the colors for a baby girl, baby boy or gender-neutral celebration!

Yield: 20 cookies total (5 footie pajamas, 5 stars, 5 body suits and 5 baby carriages)

TO MAKE THIS PLATTER YOU'LL NEED

- 1 batch Foolproof Cut-Out Cookie dough (page 12)
- 1 batch Royal Icing (page 14)
- Icing colors (I used Chefmaster, see "Colors by the Ounce")

CUTTERS

- Footie Pajama cookie cutter
- Baby Carriage cookie cutter
- Star cookie cutter
- Body Suit cookie cutter

TIPS AND TOOLS

- 6 tips #2
- 2 tips #1
- 1 Wilton tip #301 (optional, see Step 4 in the Footie Pajama)
- 1 Ateco tip #44 (optional, see Step 4 in the Footie Pajama)
- 6 couplers
- 11 icing bags (6 icing bags for piping and 5 bags, or bottles, for flooding)
- Parchment paper
- Cookie sheets
- Toothpick or scribe
- Gold star candies (I like the Wilton brand)
- Yellow food-safe marker (optional)

STEP 1: PREP THE COOKIES

Use the Foolproof Cut-Out Cookie Recipe on page 12 to bake your cookies, cutting five of each cookie cutter design.

STEP 2: MIX THE ICING AND PREP THE COLORS

Use the Royal Icing Recipe on page 14 to mix a single batch of icing (18 to 20 ounces [530 to 600 ml]). Divide the icing into bowls and make the six icing colors according to the guide below (refer to page 18 for tips on coloring icing).

STEP 3: ADJUST THE ICING CONSISTENCY

When you're ready to decorate, adjust the consistency of the different icing colors to create piping icing and flooding icing according to the amounts below. For a refresher on icing consistencies, see page 16. Once the icing colors and consistencies are ready, prep them into piping bags, referring to the individual decorating tutorials for details.

COLORS BY THE OUNCE

- **Gold Icing:** 4 oz (120 ml) (1 oz [30 ml] for pipe and 3 oz [90 ml] for flood)
- **Light Royal Blue Icing:** 5 oz (150 ml) (1 oz [30 ml] for pipe and 4 oz [120 ml] for flood)
- **Royal Blue Icing:** 3 oz (90 ml) (1 oz [30 ml] for pipe and 2 oz [60 ml] for flood)
- **White Icing:** 3 oz (90 ml) (1 oz [30 ml] for pipe and 2 oz [60 ml] for flood)
- **Bakers Rose Icing:** 4 oz (120 ml) (1 oz [30 ml] for pipe and 3 oz [90 ml] for flood)
- **Black Icing:** 1 oz (30 ml) (for pipe only)

Now that your cookies and icing are prepped, it's time to decorate! Use the instructions for each individual cookie to help decorate this Twinkle, Twinkle Little Star cookie platter!

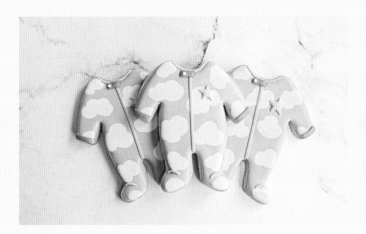

Sweet Dreams Footie Pajama Cookie

Baby snuggles are the best. And snuggly footie pajama cookies are a definite second best! This footie pajama is cute in a variety of patterns and colors, but to go with the Twinkle, Twinkle theme, we are going to create a very cool wet-on-wet cloud pattern.

Yield: *5 cookies*

OUTLINE THE COOKIES

Step 1: Outline the pajama area with light royal blue piping icing and a tip #2.

FLOOD THE COOKIES

Now, flood the cookie. Since this is the feature cookie of this set, allow a little extra time in your cookie plan to create the wet-on-wet cloud pattern on the pajamas. I tested several approaches to create this cloud pattern and found this way to be the easiest with the best results—the clouds really held their shape.

Step 2: The first step to creating this pattern is to flood the light royal blue background. We will be adding more icing to create the clouds, so don't overdo this blue base layer, otherwise the icing might overflow the outline. Also, when doing a wet-on-wet technique, be sure to use the flood icing, not the piping icing. The icing consistencies need to match, so the icings melt into each other to create a flat surface for piping details on top.

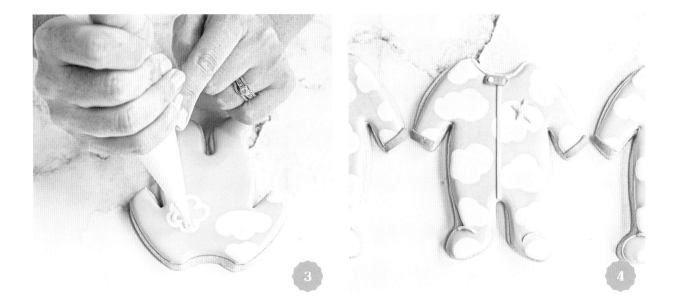

Step 3: Once the base layer is flooded, use the white flooding icing to create the clouds. Using the flood icing, create the shape of the cloud first (the outline), then flood in the cloud completely. Don't hesitate to add a little extra white to cover up any blue that's still peeking through. There is no wrong way to do this. Just have fun wiggling and flooding the cloud shapes! I like to have some full clouds on the front of the pajamas and some partial clouds on the sleeves, feet and sides to make the pattern look complete.

Stop and dry the iced cookies in front of a fan for 1 hour before adding the details. It's helpful to work in groups of cookies. While one tray is drying, move onto the next tray. See my notes on decorating in an assembly line on page 25.

ADD THE DETAILS

Step 4: Use the gold piping icing and a tip #1 to pipe a star on the right chest. Pipe the star like you would draw it. Then use the gold flood icing to fill it in, flooding over the lines. A star candy could also be used for this detail.

Add the zipper using the light royal blue piping icing and the tip #301. Keep the opening of the tip horizontal so the icing comes out flat. No tip #301? No worries! You can easily pipe this line with a tip #2 and it will look just as cute!

Use light royal blue icing and a tip #2 to pipe a line for the collar. Add a piped line with light royal blue piping icing and a tip #2 at the foot to create a small detail that looks like a fold in the fabric. Add the cuffs and the snap using royal blue piping icing and the tip #44. I love this tip because it pipes a wide stripe of icing quickly. If you don't have a tip #44, you can use tip #2 to pipe the small section and then flood in that area. Use white piping icing and a tip #2 to add a small dot on the snap.

Baby Carriage with Sparkling Stars Cookie

The gold star details on the baby carriage make this cookie a standout on the platter! Keep the details simple with icing loops. This cookie has a great space that can be personalized with the baby's name if you'd like!

Yield: *5 cookies*

OUTLINE THE COOKIES

Step 1: Outline the wheels first using white piping icing and a tip #2. To help guide my piping, I traced circles using a coupler and a yellow food safe marker (I like the brand FooDoodler). Pipe the spokes of the wheels. I piped a center vertical line and then piped an "X" on top. While the icing is still wet, add a gold star candy to the center. These are available in a variety of places and brands, but I like Wilton gold stars the best.

Then, using royal blue piping icing and a tip #2, outline the body of the carriage. Pipe the line across the top of the carriage and pipe around the wheels.

Pipe the white shade using white piping icing and a tip #2. Only pipe the first three scallops to allow a bit of room for the dangling gold star.

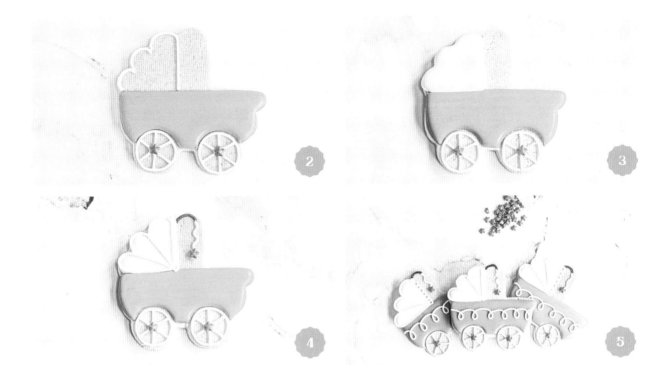

Step 2: Flood the body of the carriage with royal blue flood icing.

Stop and dry the iced cookies in front of a fan for 1 hour before flooding the next section.

Step 3: Flood the shade on the carriage using white flood icing.

Stop and dry the iced cookies in front of a fan for 30 minutes before adding the details.

ADD THE DETAILS

Step 4: Start with decorating the top of the carriage. Pipe the accordion lines on the shade using white piping icing and a tip #2. Add a scalloped line to the front edge of the shade for a frilly and fun detail. Pipe a short black scallop with piping icing and a tip #2. Then pipe a wavy line with white icing and a tip #2. While the white icing is still wet, add a gold star candy to the end so it looks like it is dangling down to entertain the baby.

Step 5: Now let's finish the main body of the carriage. Use white piping icing and a tip #2 to add six loops. Keep your tip up and off the surface of the icing and allow the icing loops to fall onto the surface of the icing. Before you jump onto the cookie, practice your loops on a piece of parchment paper. Check out the piping practice sheet on page 146.

Twinkle, Twinkle Little Star Cookie

This sweet, sleepy star reminds me of a character my girls loved to watch before bed when they were little. You'll love making this uncomplicated cookie, and it's also an essential part of the Twinkle, Twinkle Little Star theme!

Yield: *5 cookies*

OUTLINE THE COOKIES

Step 1: Outline the star cookie using gold piping icing and a tip #2.

FLOOD THE COOKIES

Step 2: Flood the star generously using gold flood icing.

Stop and dry the iced cookies in front of a fan for 1 hour before adding the details.

ADD THE DETAILS

Step 3: Pipe the face using black icing and a tip #1. I like to keep the eyes wide and center the smile. Add six short lines to create the eyelashes.

Step 4: Add rosy cheeks using the pink flood icing. Just a quick dot is enough.

Snuggly Body Suit Cookie

The decorating possibilities with a body suit cookie are endless. We are going to create a simple striped background, but any of the wet-on-wet techniques featured in this book would be great!

Yield: *5 cookies*

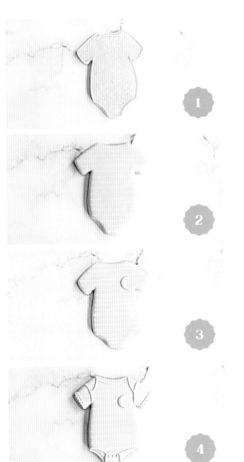

OUTLINE THE COOKIES

Step 1: Outline the body suit cookie using pink piping icing and a tip #2.

FLOOD THE COOKIES

We are going to use a wet-on-wet technique to add the stripe pattern!

Step 2: Flood in the base layer of the cookie using pink flood icing. Don't overfill the base icing layer because we are going to add more icing with the stripes. If too much is added, the icing could overflow over the outline. While the base layer is still wet, use your white flood icing, and add the white icing stripes to the pink. If you like the look of the thinner lines, make sure the opening on your white flood bag is trimmed very small, or use a tip #1 with the flood icing to have more control over the icing flow. The mini white stripes should melt into the background, creating a flat layer of icing. If the lines still look raised, pick up your cookie and give it a good shimmy to settle the icing flat!

Stop and dry the iced cookies in front of a fan for 1 hour before adding the details.

ADD THE DETAILS

Step 3: Use the gold piping icing and a tip #1 to pipe a moon on the right chest. Then, using the gold flood icing, fill it in. You could also use a star candy for this detail.

Step 4: Add detail lines to the body suit at the collar, sleeves and legs using pink icing and a tip #2. Don't forget the buttons and small scallops on the sleeves, using white piping icing and a tip #2.

Here Comes the Bride

This bridal cookie set has it all! Something old, something new, something borrowed and something blue! The three cookies from this set coordinate well, but their simply sweet designs are strong enough that they could be a stand-alone party favor at a bridal shower or wedding event. The feature cookie of this platter is the diamond ring, with both glitter and gold embellishments. The accent cookies are the wedding cake and wedding dress. The turquoise and rose pink pack a cute punch, but it would be easy to change the colors to match the wedding décor!

Yield: *21 cookies total (7 diamond rings, 7 wedding dresses and 7 wedding cakes)*

TO MAKE THIS PLATTER YOU'LL NEED

- 1 batch Foolproof Cut-Out Cookie dough (page 12)
- 1 batch Royal Icing (page 14)
- Icing colors (I used Chefmaster, see "Colors by the Ounce")

CUTTERS

- Diamond Ring cookie cutter
- Dress cookie cutter
- Wedding Cake cookie cutter

TIPS AND TOOLS

- 1 tip #1
- 4 tips #2
- 2 Wilton tips #13
- 1 Ateco tip #44
- 5 couplers
- 7 icing bags (5 icing bags for piping and 2 bags, or bottles, for flooding)
- Parchment paper
- Cookie sheets
- Toothpick or scribe
- Shot glass (or small traceable circle)
- Yellow food marker (optional)
- Edible Diamondust glitter (optional)
- Small dust pump (optional)
- Edible gold Crystal Colors dust (optional)
- Dust pump or small food-safe brush
- 1 to 2 tsp (5 to 10 ml) alcohol, lemon extract or water (to mix with the gold dust)
- Eyedropper

STEP 1: PREP THE COOKIES

Use the Foolproof Cut-Out Cookie Recipe on page 12 to bake your cookies, cutting seven of each cookie cutter design.

STEP 2: MIX THE ICING AND PREP THE COLORS

Use the Royal Icing Recipe on page 14 to mix a single batch of icing (18 to 20 ounces [530 to 600 ml]). Divide the icing into bowls and make the five icing colors according to the guide below (refer to page 18 for tips on coloring icing).

STEP 3: ADJUST THE ICING CONSISTENCY

When you're ready to decorate, adjust the consistency of the different icing colors to create piping icing and flooding icing (including the stiff piping icing needed for the two rose icing colors) according to the amounts below. For a refresher on making icing consistencies, see page 16. Once the icing colors and consistencies are ready, prep them into piping bags, referring to the individual decorating tutorials for details.

COLORS BY THE OUNCE

- Gold Icing: 3 oz (90 ml) (1 oz [30 ml] for pipe and 2 oz [60 ml] for flood)
- White Icing: 12 oz (360 ml) (2 oz [60 ml] for pipe and 10 oz [300 ml] for flood)
- Pastel Rose Pink Icing: 1 oz (30 ml) (for *stiff* pipe only)
- Dark Rose Pink Icing: 1 oz (30 ml) (for *stiff* pipe only)
- Pastel Turquoise Icing: 1 oz (30 ml) (for pipe only)

Now that your cookies and icing are prepped, it's time to decorate! Use the instructions for each individual cookie to help decorate this Here Comes the Bride cookie platter!

Diamond Ring with Lots of Bling Cookie

Diamonds are a cookie lover's best friend! These sweet cookies have all the bells and whistles to please the pickiest of brides! Check out Steps 3 and 6 to learn how to add the bling and sparkle to the cookie.

Yield: *7 cookies*

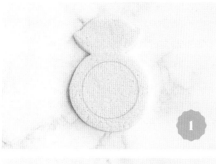

TRACE AND OUTLINE THE COOKIES

Step 1: Create a perfect circle on the diamond ring by using a thin yellow food marker to trace a 1⅞-inch (4.8-cm) circle onto the cookie. You can use an upside-down shot glass or cut a circle out of paper. This step requires a little extra effort, but it is worth it and should only take about 5 minutes if you work quickly. You can trace a second circle that is 2½ inches (6.4 cm), but I find the second circle can be freehanded using the edge of the cookie as a guide.

Step 2: Now that there are guidelines traced on the cookie, pipe the outline of the ring using gold piping icing and a tip #2. Pipe the two prong settings also using gold icing and a tip #2. Pipe the outline of the diamond using white icing and a tip #2.

FLOOD THE COOKIES

Now, let's flood the cookie in. If you choose to use the edible glitter, it makes sense to flood the white icing first to avoid getting the glitter on the gold icing areas.

Step 3: Use the white flood icing and flood the diamond. While this icing is still wet, add the edible glitter. This is optional. The cookie will look beautiful without the glitter, but this extra sparkle can be a lot of fun. I recommend finding a glitter that is FDA approved. Apply the glitter to the wet icing using a dust pump. With just a few pumps, the dust pump applies the sparkle easily and evenly. If you don't have a dust pump, you can dip a food-safe brush into the glitter and shake it onto the cookie.

Step 4: Flood in the inside of the ring using white flood icing.

Stop and dry the iced cookies in front of a fan for 1 hour before flooding in the next section. It's helpful to work in groups of cookies. While one tray is drying, move onto the next tray. See my notes on decorating in an assembly line on page 25.

Step 5: Flood in the ring using gold flood icing.

Stop and dry the iced cookies in front of a fan for 1 hour before adding the details.

ADD THE DETAILS AND METALLIC ACCENTS

Step 6: After the gold icing has dried for at least an hour, you can paint on the metallic shine. I like to use Crystal Color gold dust because it is FDA approved as edible. Mix it with grain alcohol or vodka, using a dropper to add the alcohol until the dust is liquid. If you don't have alcohol on hand, you can use lemon extract or water. I use a very small food-safe brush and paint on the gold liquid. Don't worry about any residual taste from the alcohol; the small bit in the mixture will evaporate, leaving behind only the shine.

Step 7: Pipe the diamond accents using white piping icing and a tip #1. Outline the entire diamond. Pipe a horizontal line to set off the details. Add a "W" on top of the line. Then add three more piped lines below.

Step 8: Embellish the ring with a small cluster of flowers. Hold the icing bag upright (at a 90-degree angle to the cookie), use a star tip #13 and pipe in a swirl or circular motion to create the dark rose pink rosette. Make sure the icing is stiff so it holds its shape. Then add 3 "stars" on either side using the light rose pink piping icing and a tip #13. These are quick and easy to add, just squeeze and release an itty-bitty star. To finish off the cluster, use the turquoise piping icing to pipe vines or scrolls on either side of the cluster. Pipe "C"- and "S"-shaped scrolls to wrap around the ring.

Romantic Ruffled Bridal Gown Cookie

The ruffled panel and blossoming neckline on this wedding dress cookie add an air of romance to this collection. I love the slender shape of this cutter, but these details would translate well on most wedding dress cookie cutter shapes.

Yield: *7 cookies*

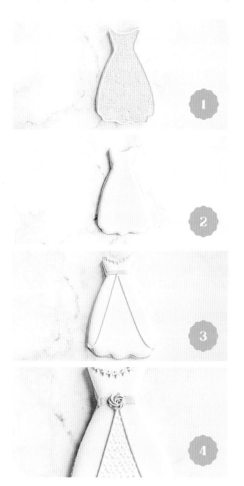

OUTLINE THE COOKIES

Step 1: Outline the dress using white piping icing and a tip #2.

FLOOD THE COOKIES

Step 2: Flood the cookie with white flood icing. Be generous with the flood icing to achieve a full look once the icing dries.

Stop and dry the iced cookies in front of a fan for 1 hour before adding the details.

ADD THE DETAILS

Step 3: Add the wide waistline using turquoise icing and the tip #44. Create the illusion of the folds in the fabric using pastel rose pink piping icing and a tip #2. Start at the center of the waistline and pipe two curving lines to form the hem of the dress. Then, switch the pastel rose pink to a tip #13. Pipe small stars at the neckline. These are small star shapes, but they look like flowers when done in a cluster.

Step 4: Fill the center section on the skirt with tons of tiny scallops to look like ruffles. Using white piping icing and the tip #1, start at the waist and work down to the hem. Use very light hand pressure while piping the scallops. Bump along, making tiny little scalloped lines. Keep the lines close together to make a gorgeous texture. Embellish the sash on the dress with a simple rosette. Using a star tip #13 and dark rose stiff icing, hold the icing bag upright (at a 90-degree angle to the cookie) and pipe a swirl in a circular motion. Make sure the icing is stiff so it holds its shape.

Happily Ever After Wedding Cake Cookie

The sweetest way to kick off "Happily Ever After" is with wedding cake. This cookie favor takes a classic wedding cake design and turns it into a handheld cookie favor! Ribbon-trimmed cake layers are the perfect way to add a pop of color, and bursts of flower clusters add a pop of texture.

Yield: *7 cookies*

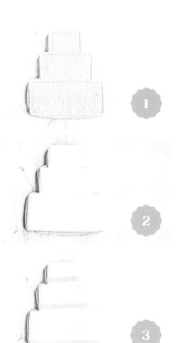

OUTLINE THE COOKIES

Step 1: Outline the cookie using white piping icing and a tip #2. Even though the entire cake will be flooded, rather than individual layers, pipe each layer to establish squared edges on the cake.

FLOOD THE COOKIES

Step 2: Flood the entire cake cookie. Be generous! Flood over the horizontal piped lines between the layers.

Stop and dry the iced cookies in front of a fan for 1 hour before adding the details.

ADD THE DETAILS

Step 3: Pipe the ribbon using turquoise and the tip #44. Keep the tip wide and flat when piping. Be extra careful to keep the lines level.

Step 4: Add the details to each cake layer using the white piping icing and the tip #1. Take your time as you stretch out the piped lines between each loop. A quick circle motion helps to drop the tiny loop. About five loops fit on each line. Practice on a piece of parchment or use the practice sheet found on page 146. Then pipe vertical lines across the middle layer. Finish off the top cake layer with polka dots.

Step 5: Add clusters of stars to each layer using the pastel and dark rose pink piping icing and a tip #13. Start the cluster with one star in the middle. Then add four of each color around the outside. On the third tier of the cake, add one extra layer to make the cluster more proportionate to the space. See the final cookie picture at the top of the page for a visual of these details.

Winter Holiday Festivities

Winter is the best season to bake and decorate cookies! Not only do the ovens warm our homes, but the exchange of cookies around the holidays warms our hearts.

Nothing is better than nibbling a cookie by the fire or enjoying one with a hot cup of cocoa. In this chapter, the Comfy and Cozy Winter set (page 53) will teach you how to create three cookies with a beautiful cool icing palette. Then it's time to start baking up memories in the kitchen with holiday cookies. The characters from the Classic Christmas Faces set (page 61) will be the highlight of the cookie plate on Christmas Eve. Or make the Folk Christmas cookies (page 69) as an artisan platter to share at holiday parties or a cookie exchange.

Comfy and Cozy Winter

This gorgeous winter set requires only three food gel colors—burgundy, navy and white. Minimum color prep always means maximum cookie fun! Plus, a streamlined color palette creates a cohesive color plan. The feature cookie of this platter is the knit sweater with lots of luscious texture. The accent cookies are the snowflakes and hot cocoa mugs. You can make these cookies as a set or just pick one design to keep things simple. Just keep in mind that the feature sweater cookie has more steps and is the most time-consuming to create.

Yield: 18 full-size cookies total (6 mugs, 6 sweaters and 6 large snowflakes)

TO MAKE THIS PLATTER YOU'LL NEED

- 1 batch Foolproof Cut-Out Cookie dough (page 12)
- 1 batch Royal Icing (page 14)
- Icing colors (I used Chefmaster, see "Colors by the Ounce")

CUTTERS

- Sweater cookie cutter
- Mug cookie cutter
- Large Snowflake cookie cutter

TIPS AND TOOLS

- 5 tips #2
- 5 couplers
- 10 icing bags (5 icing bags for piping and 5 bags, or bottles, for flooding)
- Parchment paper
- Cookie sheets
- Toothpick or scribe

STEP 1: PREP THE COOKIES

Use the Foolproof Cut-Out Cookie Recipe on page 12 to bake your cookies, cutting six of each cookie cutter design.

STEP 2: MIX THE ICING AND PREP THE COLORS

Use the Royal Icing Recipe on page 14 to mix a single batch of icing (18 to 20 ounces [530 to 600 ml]). Divide the icing into bowls and make the 5 icing colors according to the guide below. When making two shades of the same color, make the dark shade first. Then remove 1 to 3 tsp (5 to 15 ml) of the icing and add it to the white icing to make the lighter shade. You could also just add 1 or 2 drops of color to make the pastel shade and 5 to 6 drops to make the deeper color.

STEP 3: ADJUST THE ICING CONSISTENCY

When you're ready to decorate, adjust the consistency of the different icing colors to create piping icing and flooding icing according to the amounts below. For a refresher on making icing consistencies, see page 16. Once the icing colors and consistencies are ready, prep them into piping bags, referring to the individual decorating tutorials for details.

COLORS BY THE OUNCE

- Burgundy Icing: 5 oz (150 ml) (1 oz [30 ml] for pipe and 4 oz [120 ml] for flood)
- Light Burgundy Icing: 2 oz (60 ml) (1 oz [30 ml] for pipe and 1 oz [30 ml] for flood)
- Navy Icing: 4 oz (120 ml) (1 oz [30 ml] for pipe and 3 oz [90 ml] for flood)
- Light Navy Icing: 6 oz (180 ml) (1 oz [30 ml] for pipe and 5 oz [150 ml] for flood)
- White Icing: 3 oz (90 ml) (1 oz [30 ml] for pipe and 2 oz [60 ml] for flood)

Now that your cookies and icing are prepped, it's time to decorate! Use the instructions for each individual cookie to help decorate this Comfy and Cozy Winter cookie platter!

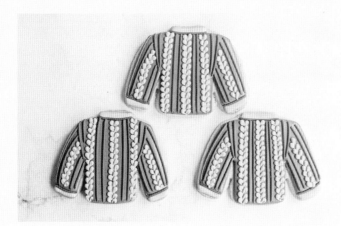

Cozy Knit Sweater Cookie

The texture of the knit makes this an impressive *and* delicious sweater cookie! Plan a little extra decorating time for this cookie to account for the extra piping of all the beautiful details.

Yield: *6 cookies*

OUTLINE THE COOKIES

Step 1: First outline the sides of the sweater using burgundy piping icing and a tip #2. Start the armpit ½ inch (1.3 cm) from the edge of the cookie to give the arms of the sweater a more distinct shape. As you work the outline around the shape of the sweater, be sure to allow a little room for the collar and the cuffs on the sweater. Leave ⅛ inch (3 mm) for those small sections. Then outline the collar and cuff sections using the light burgundy icing and a tip #2.

FLOOD THE COOKIES

Step 2: Flood the main section of the sweater using the burgundy flood icing.

Stop and dry the iced cookies in front of a fan for 1 hour before flooding the next sections. It's helpful to work in groups of cookies. While one tray is drying, move onto the next tray. See my notes on decorating in an assembly line on page 25.

Step 3: Flood the collar and cuffs with the light burgundy flood icing.

Stop and dry the iced cookies in front of a fan for 30 minutes before adding the details.

ADD THE DETAILS

Step 4: Pipe a line across the top of the sweater and at the cuffs using burgundy piping icing and a tip #2.

Step 5: Start the knit pattern in the center of the sweater using light burgundy piping icing and a tip #2. The knit texture is nothing more than an overlapping series of hearts. I like to pipe each tiny heart as two teardrops, starting at the wide areas and matching up the tails. When the hearts are piped close together and overlap, they create the illusion of a cable-knit texture.

Step 6: Pipe two burgundy lines on either side of the center knit area using burgundy piping icing and a tip #2.

Step 7: Then add one more row of knit cables (overlapping hearts) on both sides of the sweater using the light burgundy piping icing with a tip #2. Pipe two burgundy lines at the top of both shoulders using a tip #2.

Step 8: Add a centered line of overlapping hearts on each sleeve using the light burgundy piping icing and a tip #2. Add two lines on either side using the burgundy piping icing and a tip #2.

Steamy Hot Cocoa with Whipped Cream Cookie

Tall stacks of whipped cream are a wintertime essential. They make this hot cocoa mug cookie look extra decadent!

Yield: *6 cookies*

OUTLINE THE COOKIES

Step 1: Outline the mug using navy piping icing and a tip #2. Use white piping icing and a tip #2 to section out the layers of whipped cream. Use the shape and curve of the cookie to guide the outlines. Three layers of whipped cream fit well with this design.

FLOOD THE COOKIES

Step 2: Flood the mug using navy flood icing. Flood the center layer of whipped cream using white flood icing.

Stop and dry the iced cookies in front of a fan for 1 hour before flooding the next sections.

Step 3: Flood the top and bottom sections of the whipped cream layers using white flood icing.

Stop and dry the iced cookies in front of a fan for 30 minutes before adding the details.

ADD THE DETAILS

Step 4: Pipe a top and bottom line to decorate the mug using burgundy, light burgundy and light navy piping icings and tips #2. Add a white line at the bottom using piping icing and a tip #2. Pipe scallops across the top of the mug using the white piping icing and a tip #2 (I find seven scallop "humps" fit well in this space).

Step 5: Add a dot of light navy at each point of the scallop to finish.

Wintery Snowflake Cookie

Use a combination of loops, lines and hearts to make pretty snowflake cookies. Just like each snowflake is unique, you can switch it up and try new combos of icing accents to create a variety of designs.

Yield: *6 cookies*

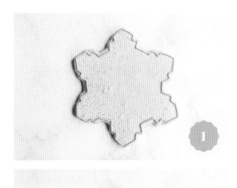

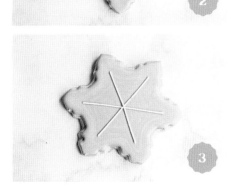

OUTLINE THE COOKIES

Step 1: Outline the snowflake using light navy piping icing and a tip #2.

FLOOD THE COOKIES

Step 2: Flood the entire snowflake using light navy flood icing.

Stop and dry the iced cookies in front of a fan for 1 hour before adding the details.

ADD THE DETAILS

Step 3: Pipe a line down the middle using white piping icing and a tip #2. Then crisscross icing on the center line, adding two piped lines or an "X" over the center line using white piping icing and a tip #2.

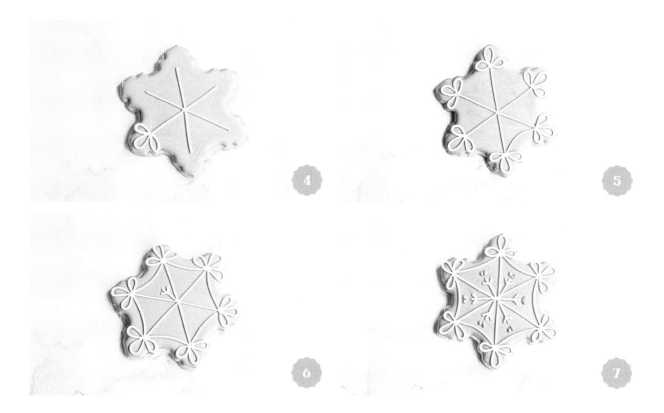

Step 4: Add three loops to the end of one line using white piping icing and a tip #2. If you'd like, practice making loops on parchment paper or using the practice sheet on page 146 before making them directly on the cookie.

Step 5: Repeat to create the loops on the ends of all the other lines.

Step 6: String a line between the ends of each line using white piping icing and a tip #2. Pipe six small lines in the center of the snowflake. Pipe a small "v" shape to add an extra snowflake detail using white piping icing and a tip #2.

Step 7: Pipe a small heart at the tip of each short line using the light burgundy piping icing and a tip #2. Pipe the hearts as two teardrops, using strong hand pressure to start at the wide areas and then easing off to pull out the tail. Match up the tails to create the heart shape. Not only does this add a pop of color, but it also coordinates well with the sweater design!

Classic Christmas Faces

Christmas is the one day of the year our family eats cookies for breakfast! Some of our favorite designs to decorate (and enjoy!) include the cute faces of the Christmas season, like Santa, his elf and a red-nosed reindeer. The feature cookie of this platter is the Santa, but because it's Christmas, the other two cookies on this platter are a little more involved than basic accent cookies. You can find a template for Santa and his elf on page 145. You can make these cookies as a set or just pick one design to keep things simple. Just keep in mind that the feature Santa cookie has more steps and is the most time-consuming to create.

Yield: *18 cookies total (6 Santas, 6 reindeer and 6 elves)*

TO MAKE THIS PLATTER YOU'LL NEED

- 1 batch Foolproof Cut-Out Cookie dough (page 12)
- 1 batch Royal Icing (page 14)
- Icing colors (I used Chefmaster, see "Colors by the Ounce")

CUTTERS (SEE NOTE)

- Whimsical Santa Face cookie cutter from Ann Clark Cookie Cutters
- Elf Face cookie cutter from Ann Clark Cookie Cutters
- Reindeer Face cookie cutter from Ann Clark Cookie Cutters

TIPS AND TOOLS

- 6 tips #2
- 6 couplers
- 11 icing bags (6 icing bags for piping and 5 bags, or bottles, for flooding)
- Parchment paper
- Cookie sheets
- Toothpick or scribe
- Yellow food marker
- Santa and elf templates (on page 145)
- White nonpareils
- Leaf (or holly) sprinkles
- Tweezers (optional)
- Crystal Color carnation pink dust, to blush the cheeks
- Food-safe brush

STEP 1: PREP THE COOKIES

Use the Foolproof Cut-Out Cookie Recipe on page 12 to bake your cookies, cutting six of each cookie cutter design.

STEP 2: MIX THE ICING AND PREP THE COLORS

Use the Royal Icing Recipe on page 14 to mix a single batch of icing (18 to 20 ounces [530 to 600 ml]). Divide icing into bowls and make the six icing colors according to the guide on the following page.

Create custom skin tones for your Santa and elf cookies! A wide range of shades come from one bottle. Typically I use sienna for lighter skin colors. Creating this color only takes a scant dot of gel. For brown skin tones, I use buckeye brown for light, medium and dark colors. You can deepen the color by adding more drops of color. You can even mix both gels together. For a medium creamy skin tone, try mixing sienna with buckeye brown.

To reduce the number of icing colors required for this set, I used the same brown for the elf's hair as the brown on the reindeer. However, you can customize your elf's hair color by exploring different shades of brown, black, golden yellow or red (orange) gels.

STEP 3: ADJUST THE ICING CONSISTENCY

When you're ready to decorate, adjust the consistency of the different icing colors to create piping icing and flooding icing according to the amounts on the following page. For a refresher on making icing consistencies, see page 16. Once the icing colors and consistencies are ready, prep them into piping bags, referring to the individual decorating tutorials for details.

(Continued)

Classic Christmas Faces (Continued)

COLORS BY THE OUNCE

- White Icing: 6 oz (180 ml) (1 oz [30 ml] for pipe and 5 oz [150 ml] for flood)
- Brown Icing: 4 oz (120 ml) (1 oz [30 ml] for pipe and 3 oz [90 ml] for flood)
- Leaf Green Icing: 4 oz (120 ml) (1 oz [30 ml] for pipe and 3 oz [90 ml] for flood)
- Skin Tone Icing (Sienna, Buckeye Brown or a Combo): 3 oz (90 ml) (1 oz [30 ml] for pipe and 2 oz [60 ml] for flood)
- Christmas Red Icing: 2 oz (60 ml) (1 oz [30 ml] for pipe and 1 oz [30 ml] for flood)
- Black Icing: 1 oz (30 ml) (for pipe only)

Now that your cookies and icing are prepped, it's time to decorate! Use the instructions for each individual cookie to help decorate this Classic Christmas Faces cookie platter!

A NOTE ABOUT USING THE TEMPLATES FOR THIS COOKIE SET:

The templates on page 145 were designed to fit the Ann Clark cookie cutters. You can copy the page, cut out the template and trace the guides onto the cookie with a yellow food marker. However, if using a similar, but not exact cookie cutter, you may need to adjust the design to fit your cutter shape. Use the supplied templates as inspiration. Trace your cutter on a piece of paper. Draw the design that fits your cutter. Then cut and trace the template onto the cookie.

Jolly Santa Face Cookie

Twinkling eyes, cheeks like roses and his mustache and beard like snow, this Santa cookie is so much fun to bring to life. This cookie is dripping with lots of details, so plan a little extra decorating time to get him done.

Yield: *6 cookies*

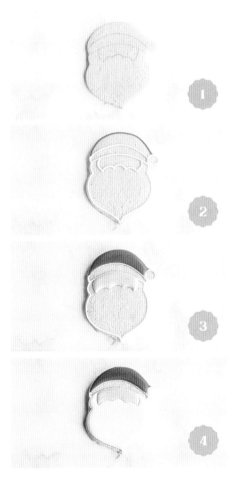

TRACE THE TEMPLATE ON THE COOKIES

Step 1: Cut out the section of the template to trace onto the cookie. For this project, cut out the fur from Santa's hat and the outline of his face. Use a light-colored food marker, like yellow, to trace around the edges of the template.

OUTLINE THE COOKIES

Step 2: Pipe the outline of the fur and Santa's face using white piping icing and a tip #2. Following the shape of the cookie, outline the beard and the pom-pom using white piping icing and a tip #2. Outline the top of the hat using red piping icing and a tip #2.

FLOOD THE COOKIES

Step 3: Flood Santa's face using the skin tone flood icing (shown here is light sienna, see page 61 for tips on adjusting skin tone colors). Fill in the hat using red flood icing.

Stop and dry the iced cookies in front of a fan for 30 minutes before flooding the next sections. It's helpful to work in groups of cookies. While one tray is drying, move onto the next tray. See my notes on decorating in an assembly line on page 25.

Step 4: Flood the pom-pom and beard using white flood icing.

Stop and dry the iced cookies in front of a fan for 30 minutes before flooding the next section.

(Continued)

Step 5: Flood the fur on Santa's hat using white flood icing. While the icing is wet, set the cookie on a coffee filter and pour white nonpareils on the wet icing. The nonpareils will stick to the wet icing. The coffee filter will catch any sprinkles that don't stick to the icing and they can be easily poured back into their container. Add Santa's nose using the skin tone flood icing.

Stop and dry the iced cookies in front of a fan for 30 minutes before adding the mustache.

CREATE THE MUSTACHE

Step 6: Use white piping icing with a tip #2 to outline Santa's mustache. Start at the side of the nose and follow the line of his cheek. Bring the outline out past his face and curl up. Finish the bottom of the mustache with a curved line back to the center of the bottom of the nose. Repeat on the other side.

Step 7: Fill in the mustache using white flood icing.

Stop and dry the iced cookies in front of a fan for 30 minutes before adding the details.

ADD THE DETAILS

Step 8: Make Santa's rosy cheeks using the edible carnation pink dust and a food-safe brush. Add a piped line for Santa's mouth using the skin tone piping icing and a tip #2. Then add a tiny dot of red flood icing inside the mouth. Tap the red icing into place using a scribe tool.

Step 9: Add the final details to Santa's hat and face. Add the eyes with two dots of black piping icing and a tip #2. Add eyebrows using white piping icing and a tip #2. Give the brow a bushy look with four overlapping dots of icing (like a bead border). Add a swirl on the pom-pom using red icing and a tip #2. Using tweezers, add two candy sprinkle leaves for holly with a dot of icing on the back of each leaf. Pipe three dots using red piping icing and a tip #2 for the berries.

Elf Face Cookie

Santa can't make all the toys by himself; he needs an elf to help! This cute elf cookie can be freehanded, but a template is provided on page 145 in case tracing the lines for the face is helpful.

Yield: *6 cookies*

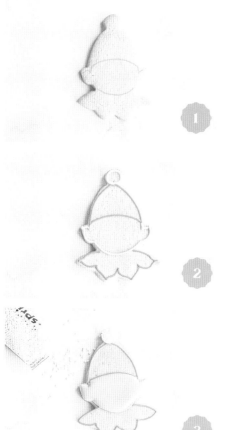

TRACE THE TEMPLATE ON THE COOKIES

Step 1: For this project, cut out the elf template, then cut out the middle face section to use for tracing. Make the cuts exact to get a precise outline on the cookie. Use a light-colored food marker, like yellow, to trace around the edges of the template.

OUTLINE THE COOKIES

Step 2: Using white piping icing and a tip #2, outline the pom-pom as a small circle on the top of the hat section. Using the traced yellow lines as a guide, pipe the outline of the elf hat using green piping icing and a tip #2. Then outline the face using the skin tone piping icing (shown here is light sienna, see page 61 for tips on adjusting skin tone colors) and a tip #2. Pipe the collar using green piping icing and a tip #2.

FLOOD THE COOKIES

Step 3: Set the cookie on a coffee filter. Fill in the pom-pom with white flood icing. Immediately, while the icing is still wet, sprinkle on the white nonpareils. Then fill in the elf's face using the skin tone flood icing.

Stop and dry the iced cookies in front of a fan for 30 minutes before flooding the next sections.

(Continued)

Step 4: Next, create the striped hat and the polka-dotted collar using wet-on-wet techniques (see page 23 for tips on wet-on-wet piping). Flood the hat using green icing. Take care not to overfill the base icing because a second color will be added. While the green icing is still wet, add red flood icing stripes. It is helpful to make sure the opening on the red icing bag is small to allow for the most control over the icing flow, keeping the stripes thin. You can also put a tip #1 on your red flood icing bag to have control over the size of the opening.

Use a wet-on-wet technique on the elf's collar. First, fill in the collar using green flood icing. While the icing is still wet, add red dots. Keep your wet-on-wet dots round by allowing a dot of icing to drop onto the surface, don't dip the tip of the bag into the icing.

Stop and dry the iced cookies in front of a fan for 30 minutes before flooding the next section.

Step 5: Outline the elf's hair using brown icing and a tip #2. I used the same brown icing color that is used for the reindeer, but if you'd like you can adjust to the hair color of your choice.

Step 6: Fill in the hair using brown flood icing (or flood icing for the hair color of your choice).

Stop and dry the iced cookies in front of a fan for 30 minutes before adding the details.

ADD THE DETAILS

Step 7: Blush the cheeks using the edible carnation pink dust and a food-safe brush. Add a bead border (overlapping teardrops of icing) to the base of the hat and pom-poms on the collar using white piping icing and a tip #2. For more practice with icing accents, check out the piping practice sheet on page 146. Add eyes and a side smile using black piping icing and a tip #2. Add a nose and a squiggle for ear detail using the skin tone piping icing and a tip #2. Pipe a line between the face and the collar using red piping icing and a tip #2.

Red-Nosed Reindeer Face Cookie

The red-nosed reindeer is ready to lead the sleigh! The outlines are simpler than with the Santa and Elf cookies, so no template is needed for this cookie.

Yield: *6 cookies*

OUTLINE THE COOKIES

Step 1: Outline the face and ears using brown piping icing and a tip #2. Outline the antlers using white piping icing and a tip #2.

FLOOD THE COOKIES

Step 2: Flood the main section of the face using brown flood icing.

Stop and dry the iced cookies in front of a fan for 1 hour before flooding the next section.

Step 3: Fill in the antlers using white flood icing. Add the nose using red flood icing. While the icing is still wet, add a highlight (a wet-on-wet detail) using white flood icing.

Stop and dry the iced cookies in front of a fan for 30 minutes before adding the details.

ADD THE DETAILS

Step 4: Blush the checks using the edible carnation pink dust and a food-safe brush. Add a little zigzag on the top of the head for the fur detail and outlines on the ears using brown piping icing and a tip #2. Pipe eyes and a side smile using black piping icing and a tip #2.

Folk Christmas

Growing up deep in Pennsylvania Dutch culture, I have an appreciation for folk art. This set takes those beautiful patterns, colors and textures to create a unique Christmas platter. This is a bit of a deviation from the typical, whimsical cookie design and offers a more artisan collection. This platter breaks a few rules. Instead of having both a feature and accent cookie, this set is comprised of cookies with a simple outline and flood with lots of fine piping work. I hope you can find some peace as you get lost in the meditative piping work. Allow at least 1 extra hour for detailing a batch of these cookies. Check out the piping practice sheet on page 146 to gain experience creating these icing accents. Also, get creative with your own designs by combining lines, dots, zigzags, vines and loops!

Yield: 24 cookies total (6 stockings, 6 cute deer, 6 woodland trees and 6 flying doves)

TO MAKE THIS PLATTER YOU'LL NEED

- 1 batch Foolproof Cut-Out Cookie dough (page 12)
- 1 batch Royal Icing (page 14)
- Icing colors (I used Chefmaster, see "Colors by the Ounce")

CUTTERS

- Stocking cookie cutter
- Cute Deer cookie cutter
- Woodland Tree cookie cutter
- Flying Dove cookie cutter

TIPS AND TOOLS

- 6 tips #2
- 6 tips #1.5 (this is a size from the PME brand, but a PME or Wilton tip #1 will make a good substitute)
- 6 couplers
- 12 icing bags (6 icing bags for piping and 6 bags, or bottles, for flooding)
- Parchment paper
- Cookie sheets
- Toothpick or scribe

STEP 1: PREP THE COOKIES

Use the Foolproof Cut-Out Cookie Recipe on page 12 to bake your cookies, cutting six of each cookie cutter design.

STEP 2: MIX THE ICING AND PREP THE COLORS

Use the Royal Icing Recipe on page 14 to mix a single batch of icing (18 to 20 ounces [530 to 600 ml]). Divide the icing into bowls and make the six icing colors according to the guide below.

STEP 3: ADJUST THE ICING CONSISTENCY

When you're ready to decorate, adjust the consistency of the different icing colors according to the amounts below. For a refresher on making icing consistencies, see page 16. Once the icing colors and consistencies are ready, prep them into piping bags.

COLORS BY THE OUNCE

- Red Icing: 4 oz (120 ml) (1 oz [30 ml] for pipe and 3 oz [90 ml] for flood)
- Gold Icing: 3 oz (90 ml) (1 oz [30 ml] for pipe and 2 oz [60 ml] for flood)
- Royal Blue Icing: 4 oz (120 ml) (1 oz [30 ml] for pipe and 3 oz [90 ml] for flood)
- White Icing: 3 oz (90 ml) (1 oz [30 ml] for pipe and 2 oz [60 ml] for flood)
- Forest Green Icing: 3 oz (90 ml) (1 oz [30 ml] for pipe and 2 oz [60 ml] for flood)
- Light Forest Green: 3 oz (90 ml) (1 oz [30 ml] for pipe and 2 oz [60 ml] for flood)

Now that your cookies and icing are prepped, it's time to decorate! Use the instructions for each individual cookie to help decorate this Folk Christmas cookie platter!

Stitched with Love Stocking Cookie

This cookie is my favorite of the set because I love to get lost in the details. The top of the stocking features a new take on creating a knit texture in icing. Then create the interesting patterns using any combination of dashes, Xs, loops, lines, dots, zigzags and hash marks. The possibilities are endless.

Yield: *6 cookies*

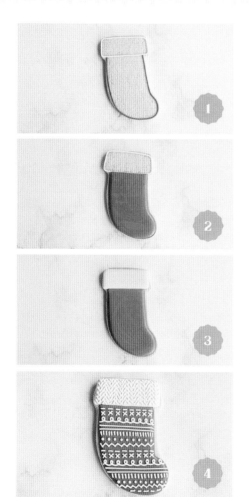

OUTLINE THE COOKIES

Step 1: Outline the top of the stocking using white piping icing and a tip #2. Outline the bottom using red icing and a tip #2.

FLOOD THE COOKIES

Step 2: Fill the main section of the stocking using red flood icing.

Stop and dry the iced cookies in front of a fan for 1 hour before flooding the next section. It's helpful to work in groups of cookies. See my notes on decorating in an assembly line on page 25.

Step 3: Fill in the top area using white flood icing.

Stop and dry the iced cookies in front of a fan for 30 minutes before adding the details.

ADD DETAILS

Tips: Use white piping icing and the tip #1.5 to add the details. The soft-peak piping icing consistency is helpful to create smooth details that hold their shape (for a refresher on icing consistencies see page 16). When using a PME tip #1.5 or PME or Wilton tip #1, it is also helpful to use light hand pressure to keep these details delicate.

Step 4: Pipe the knit texture on the top of the stocking using a "v" shape. I pipe alternating rows of v's, right-side up and upside-down. Keep the details close together to make this impressive texture. This isn't difficult to do, but all this piping does require patience. Still using the white piping icing and tip #1.5, add the details on the stocking. This is just fun! Use the photo to follow my pattern as an example or create your own. Pick a few design elements and pipe them on repeat.

Elegant Reindeer Cookie

The pop of blue from this cookie makes this platter complete. Keep the details simple on this sweet deer to balance well with the other highly textured cookies.

Yield: *6 cookies*

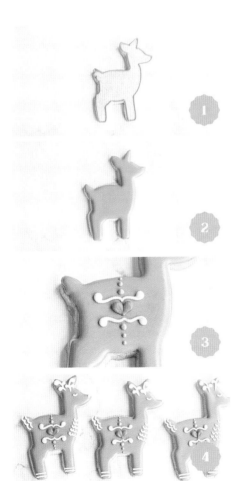

OUTLINE THE COOKIES

Step 1: Outline the entire cookie using royal blue piping icing and a tip #2.

FLOOD THE COOKIES

Step 2: Fill in the cookie using blue flood icing.

Stop and dry the iced cookies in front of a fan for 1 hour before adding the details.

ADD THE DETAILS

Step 3: Add the heart in the center of the deer using red piping icing and the tip #1.5. Pipe the hearts as two teardrops, using strong hand pressure to start at the wide areas, and then easing off to pull out the tail. Match up the tails to create the heart shape. Once that is in place, it's easier to space out and add the rest of the details. Use gold piping icing and the tip #1.5 to add two scrolls, one above and one below the heart. Add three dots using light forest green piping icing and the tip #1.5 above and below the scrolls, gradually making them smaller as you work your way to the edge of the cookie.

Step 4: Use white piping icing and the tip #1.5 to add scrolls for antlers. These are fine details, so keep your hand pressure light. Add a face, a small half circle for a closed eye and a dot for a nose. Then add the detail on the tail—two delicate scalloped lines. Pipe two lines at the hooves. Finally, add scallops on the chest. Start with one scallop and gradually increase to create the impression of fur.

Textured Woodland Tree Cookie

Adding short hash marks to this tree creates such a fun, eye-catching texture. It could represent branch details or even falling snow. Either way, I encourage you to put on your favorite holiday music and have fun building up the texture on these trees! It's so enjoyable to see the cookie come to life as the piped details are added!

Yield: *6 cookies*

OUTLINE THE COOKIES

Step 1: Outline the entire tree and pipe the wavy lines for each section using light forest green icing and a tip #2. Create four sections, two for the light green and two for the dark green.

FLOOD THE COOKIES

Step 2: On this cookie, we want a flat surface, so there is no dry time between flooding these icing areas. Flood in the sections using the light green and dark green flood icing, bumping the colors against each other to create this tree. If the wiggly line loses shape, reshape using the tip of the flood icing bag.

Stop and dry the iced cookies in front of a fan for 1 hour before adding the details.

ADD THE DETAILS

Step 3: Starting with the top and third sections of the tree, pipe short hash marks closely together using the dark forest green piping icing and the tip #1.5. Use light hand pressure to reduce points and peaks on your lines. Alternate the next row to keep the pattern varied.

Step 4: Continue the hash marks in the second and fourth sections using the light forest green and the tip #1.5. Continue down to the trunk of the tree. Save time by spacing the hash marks wider.

Flying Dove Cookie

Incorporate your favorite symbols typically used on barn signs into this dove cookie. Hearts, dots, tulips, teardrops, lines and vines are all common. I used the tulip in the center of this cookie, as it is a symbol of faith.

Yield: *6 cookies*

OUTLINE THE COOKIES

Step 1: Pipe a short white line at the bottom of the dove using white piping icing and a tip #2. Then outline the rest of the cookie using gold piping icing and a tip #2.

FLOOD THE COOKIES

Step 2: On this cookie, we want a flat surface (like on the Textured Woodland Tree Cookie, page 72), so you don't need to stop and dry the gold before flooding the white belly. Flood the gold on the dove using flood icing. Then flood the white section, bumping the white flood icing against the gold to create the flat surface.

Stop and dry the iced cookies in front of a fan for 1 hour before adding the details.

ADD THE DETAILS

Step 3: Use red piping icing and the tip #1.5 to pipe the small tulip. Pipe a teardrop of icing for the center. Add two more teardrops on the right and left to create three petals. Add a row of blue hearts using blue icing and a tip #1.5. Add the eye using blue icing. Then add five itty bitty dots (light hand pressure!) around the eye with white icing. Use the white to outline the end of the tail and add teardrops.

Step 4: Add the vine detail to the wing using dark forest green icing and the tip #1.5. Pipe the stem first. Then add teardrops of icing for the leaves—pull the tail of the teardrop to the stem to create the vine. Finally, using the light forest green piping icing, add nine thin lines to the white section of the dove.

Spring Celebrations

As the spring flowers bloom, the world comes to life around us. The shift to soft, pretty pastel icing colors is nice after using cool winter palettes and traditional Christmas colors!

In this chapter, you'll find the Valentine's Day platter (page 77), a holiday technically in the winter season, but grouped with the spring cookie sets because it has light and bright color vibes! Then, it's time to head to the farm for Easter. The Farmhouse Easter set (page 83) is a playful spring cookie platter that has a variety of wet-on-wet icing techniques. Finally, I'll share how to create a sweet pastel gardening set (page 91) perfect for Mother's Day. It features the cutest chubby boot with a really fun twist on a wet-on-wet technique.

Love Is in the Air

The sweet colors and patterns of this Love is in the Air set will take your valentine up, up and away! If you have extra dough, add in some simple heart cookies to fill out your set!

The feature cookie of this platter is the hot air balloon. The accent cookies are the clouds and Cupid's arrows. You can make these cookies as a set or just pick one design to keep things simple. Just keep in mind that the feature hot air balloon cookie is the most time-consuming to create.

Yield: *24 cookies total (8 hot air balloons, 8 clouds and 8 arrows)*

TO MAKE THIS PLATTER YOU'LL NEED

- 1 batch Foolproof Cut-Out Cookie dough (page 12)
- 1 batch Royal Icing (page 14)
- Icing colors (I used Chefmaster, see "Colors by the Ounce")

CUTTERS

- Hot Air Balloon cookie cutter
- Arrow cookie cutter
- Cloud cookie cutter

TIPS AND TOOLS

- 5 tips #2
- 2 tips #1
- 5 couplers
- 9 icing bags (5 icing bags for piping and 4 bags, or bottles, for flooding)
- Parchment paper
- Cookie sheets
- Toothpick or scribe
- Yellow food marker (optional)

STEP 1: PREP THE COOKIES

Use the Foolproof Cut-Out Cookie Recipe on page 12 to bake your cookies, cutting eight of each cookie cutter design.

STEP 2: MIX THE ICING AND PREP THE COLORS

Use the Royal Icing Recipe on page 14 to mix a single batch of icing (18 to 20 ounces [530 to 600 ml]). Divide the icing into bowls and make the five icing colors according to the guide below.

STEP 3: ADJUST THE ICING CONSISTENCY

When you're ready to decorate, adjust the consistency of the different icing colors to create piping icing and flooding icing according to the amounts below. For a refresher on making icing consistencies, see page 16. Once the colors are ready, prep them into piping bags, referring to the individual decorating tutorials for details.

COLORS BY THE OUNCE

- Sky Blue Icing: 6 oz (180 ml) (1 oz [30 ml] for pipe and 5 oz [150 ml] for flood)
- Light Deep Pink Icing: 4 oz (120 ml) (1 oz [30 ml] for pipe and 3 oz [90 ml] for flood)
- Dark Deep Pink Icing: 5 oz (150 ml) (1 oz [30 ml] for pipe and 4 oz [120 ml] for flood)
- White Icing: 4 oz (120 ml) (1 oz [30 ml] for pipe and 3 oz [90 ml] for flood)
- Black Icing: 1 oz (30 ml) (for pipe only)

Now that your cookies and icing are prepped, it's time to decorate! Use the instructions for each individual cookie to help decorate this Love Is in the Air cookie platter!

Up, Up and Away Hot Air Balloon Cookie

A ride in a hot air balloon is quite a romantic Valentine's Day vision! This Hot Air Balloon is an impressive cookie with a marbled pattern on the balloon and lots of texture on the basket.

Yield: *8 cookies*

OUTLINE THE COOKIES

Step 1: Outline the basket area with white piping icing and a tip #2. Outline the balloon with light pink piping icing and a tip #2. Allow a bit of space (about ⅓ inch [8.5 mm]) between the basket and the balloon. Follow the shape of the balloon to pipe the outline.

FLOOD THE COOKIES

Step 2: To create the beautiful pattern in the balloon, use a wet-on-wet technique called marbling. When using a wet-on-wet technique, be sure to use your flood icing, not your piping icing.

The hot air balloon pattern has three horizontal stripes of light pink and three stripes of dark pink. To evenly space lines, measure and trace lines on the cookie using a yellow food marker about ½ inch (1.3 cm) apart. While guidelines are helpful, they can also be eyeballed.

To get the pattern started, use the light pink flood icing and flood three stripes inside the balloon, allowing space for the three dark pink stripes. While the light pink flood is still wet, use the dark pink flood icing to bump up against the light pink and flood in those three sections. Clean up the seams between the icing colors by adding a single line of white flood icing.

Step 3: Immediately use the tip of your toothpick or scribe and run it down vertically through the icing stripes while the icing is still wet. It's important to work quickly and not let the icing start to set up, or raised marks from the scribe will be visible. I created a total of six vertical lines, generally following the shape of the cookie. Due to the time it takes to flood and scribe this marbled design, I suggest tackling the flooding on these hot air balloons one cookie at a time.

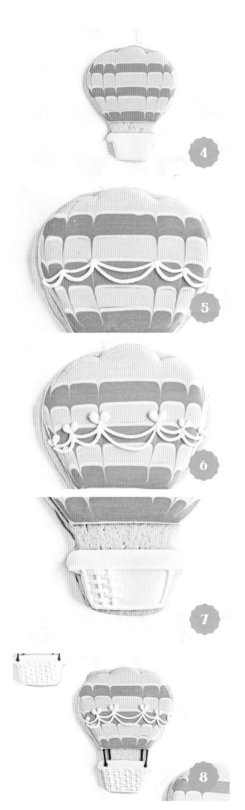

Step 4: Fill in the basket with white flood icing.

Stop and dry the iced cookies in front of a fan for 1 hour before flooding the next section. It's helpful to work in groups of cookies. While one tray is drying, move onto the next tray. See my notes on decorating in an assembly line on page 25.

ADD THE DETAILS

Step 5: Add scallops to the balloon with white piping icing and a tip #2. Pipe the center scallop first, lining up the center scallop with the center scribe lines. Then pipe two more scallops to the right and two more to the left. Pipe a second row for extra details. Create a draped look to the scallops by piping the center higher and allowing the scallops to dip down across the cookie.

Step 6: Pipe hearts above the scallops with sky blue icing and a tip #2. The heart detail is a quick and cute accent. Pipe hearts as two teardrops, using strong hand pressure to start at the wide areas, and then easing off to pull out the tail. Match up the tails to create the heart shape.

Step 7: Create the texture on the basket using white piping icing and a tip #2. It's important that the icing isn't too thin, or it will blob together and you'll lose the basket weave detail. Start the basket weave by outlining the lower portion of the basket. Then pipe a vertical line on the left side of the basket. Pipe four short horizontal lines over the top of the vertical, leaving a little space between each line. Then pipe a second vertical line, overlapping the next vertical line on the ends of the horizontal lines to enhance the illusion of the weave. Pipe another row of four short horizontal lines, offset from the first set. Continue this pattern and fill up the basket area with the vertical and horizontal lines to create the basket weave texture. When complete, pipe a small dot of icing in any open areas to fill in the design.

Step 8: Pipe black lines between the balloon and the basket. Pipe two longer lines on the edge and overlap on the front of the basket and two shorter lines on the interior to appear as though they are attached on the back of the basket.

Cupid's Arrow Cookie

Watch out when the love arrows start to fly!
Cupid himself couldn't imagine a sweeter
way to spoil a loved one than with
these cookies.

Yield: *8 cookies*

OUTLINE THE COOKIES

Step 1: Outline the tip of the arrow with dark pink icing and a tip #2.
Create a heart shape in this section to go with the Valentine's theme.
Then using white piping icing and a tip #2, outline the feather area.

FLOOD THE COOKIES

Step 2: The heart of the arrow features wet-on-wet polka dots.
Flood in the heart tip with the dark pink icing. While that base layer is
still wet, use the white flood icing (don't use the piping icing; it won't
work!), and add drops of icing to the base layer. To make mini white
dots, trim a very small opening when starting your white flood bag.
Otherwise, slip the icing bag into a clean bag with a tip #1 to get the
most control over the icing to keep those dots small. The mini white
drops should melt into the background, creating a flat layer of icing.
Flood the tail of the arrow with white flood icing.

*Stop and dry the iced cookies in front of a fan for 1 hour before adding
the details.*

ADD THE DETAILS

Step 3: Use the black piping icing and a tip #2 to pipe the cursive
word "love." If it helps, trace the cutter on a piece of paper to practice.
Pipe the word "love" going both ways, from tip to tail and also from tail
to tip. Simply flip the arrow and pipe the letters.

Step 4: Add the feather detail on the tail of the arrow. Pipe a center
line using dark pink piping icing and a tip #1. Add six equally spaced
lines on each side of the center line. Fill in the rest of the feather details
by piping five more lines using the light pink piping icing and a tip #1.

Chubby Heart Cloud Cookie

The cloud cookie is the easiest design from this set. Just a few piped details and this cookie is ready to go. The open space on the cloud is big enough if you wanted to personalize with your Valentine's name!

Yield: *8 cookies*

OUTLINE THE COOKIES

Step 1: Outline the cloud cookie using sky blue piping icing and a tip #2.

FLOOD THE COOKIES

Step 2: Flood the cloud using sky blue flood icing. With this clean design, it's important to be generous with flood icing to prevent any dips in the icing. A generous fill will create a smooth, raised look once the icing dries.

Stop and dry the iced cookies in front of a fan for 1 hour before adding the details.

ADD THE DETAILS

Step 3: Pipe two pink hearts just like in the hot air balloon tutorial. Pipe the hearts as two teardrops, using strong hand pressure to start at the wide areas, and then easing off to pull out the tail. Match up the tails to create the heart shape. I added one heart in each shade of pink. Then use white piping icing and a tip #2 to pipe a border around the cloud.

Farmhouse Easter

What's better than farm fresh eggs? Farm fresh *Easter* eggs, of course! This beautiful Easter platter has lots of farmhouse charm. The feature cookie of this platter is the barn. The accent cookies are the bunnies, spring chickens and the Easter eggs. You can make these cookies as a set or just pick one design to keep things simple.

Yield: *26 cookies (6 barns, 6 chickens, 6 bunnies and 8 eggs)*

TO MAKE THIS PLATTER YOU'LL NEED

- 1 batch Foolproof Cut-Out Cookie dough (page 12)
- 1 batch Royal Icing (page 14)
- Icing colors (I used Chefmaster, see "Colors by the Ounce")

CUTTERS

- Barn cookie cutter
- Chicken cookie cutter
- Bunny Peep cookie cutter
- 2.5" (6.3-cm) Egg cookie cutter

TIPS AND TOOLS

- 7 tips #2
- 2 tips #1
- 1 Wilton tip #13
- 7 couplers
- 14 icing bags (7 icing bags for piping and 7 bags, or bottles, for flooding)
- Parchment paper
- Cookie sheets
- Toothpick or scribe

STEP 1: PREP THE COOKIES

Use the Foolproof Cut-Out Cookie Recipe on page 12 to bake your cookies, cutting six barns, six chickens, six bunny shapes and eight eggs.

STEP 2: MIX THE ICING AND PREP THE COLORS

Use the Royal Icing Recipe on page 14 to mix a single batch of icing (18 to 20 ounces [530 to 600 ml]). Divide the icing into bowls and make the eight icing colors according to the guide below. Since we're using pastels, add 1 drop of food gel to keep each color light. I used a very small dot for the light golden yellow, and larger dot for the darker golden yellow.

STEP 3: ADJUST THE ICING CONSISTENCY

When you're ready to decorate, adjust the consistency of the different icing colors to create piping icing and flooding icing according to the amounts below. For a refresher on making icing consistencies, see page 16. Once the colors are ready, prep them into piping bags.

COLORS BY THE OUNCE

- White Icing: 4 oz (120 ml) (1 oz [30 ml] for pipe and 3 oz [90 ml] for flood)
- Pastel Turquoise Icing: 4 oz (120 ml) (1 oz [30 ml] for pipe and 3 oz [90 ml] for flood)
- Pastel Mint Green Icing: 2 oz (60 ml) (½ oz [15 ml] for pipe and 1½ oz [45 ml] for flood)
- Pastel Bakers Rose Icing: 3 oz (90 ml) (1 oz [30 ml] for pipe and 2 oz [60 ml] for flood)
- Dark Bakers Rose Icing: 1 oz (30 ml) (for pipe only)
- Black Icing: 1 oz (30 ml) (½ oz [15 ml] for pipe and ½ oz [15 ml] for flood)
- Pastel Golden Yellow Icing: 3 oz (90 ml) (1 oz [30 ml] for pipe and 2 oz [60 ml] for flood)
- Golden Yellow Icing: 1 oz (30 ml) (for flood only)

Now that your cookies and icing are prepped, it's time to decorate! Use the instructions over the next pages to decorate each cookie.

Farm Fresh Easter Eggs Barn Cookie

I love to get playful with words on cookies. Mix up the fonts and icing colors to make this the playful centerpiece of the platter.

Yield: *6 cookies*

OUTLINE THE COOKIES

Step 1: Outline the roof of the barn with black piping icing and a tip #2. Use the shape of the cookie to guide the piped lines.

Outline the main structure of the barn with turquoise piping icing and a tip #2.

FLOOD THE COOKIES

Step 2: Flood in the barn with the turquoise flood icing.

Stop and dry the iced cookies in front of a fan for 1 hour before flooding the next section. It's helpful to work in groups of cookies. While one tray is drying move onto the next tray. See my notes on decorating in an assembly line on page 25.

Step 3: Flood in the roof with the black flood icing.

Stop and dry the iced cookies in front of a fan for 30 minutes before adding the details.

ADD THE DETAILS

Step 4: Add the text to the barn. Don't be intimidated to pipe words on cookies! Icing consistency is key. Make sure you are using the soft-peak piping icing as described on page 16. If the icing is too thick or stiff, it will be hard to pipe smooth letters. If the icing is too thin, the letters won't hold their shape.

Before piping on the cookie, I like to visually see how the words will look on the cookie. I sketch or print a sample on paper and match it up with the cutter to make sure the text fits well in the space. I have also piped directly on the paper, over the sample, to practice before jumping onto the cookie. Pay attention to spacing. For this cookie, pipe the word "Easter" first in the dark bakers rose icing with a tip #2. It is centered on the cookie.

Step 5: Once you have piped the printed word "Easter," use the black piping icing and a tip #1 to add the cursive words "farm fresh" above and "eggs" below.

Step 6: Using the various colors of piping icing and a tip #2, add eggs at the base of the barn. Three eggs fit well on each side.

Step 7: Add teardrops of green icing for the grass. This adds a cute pop of color and texture! Then pipe vertical lines on the barn to create wood panels using turquoise piping icing and a tip #1. Finish the cookie by piping black lines on the roof using black piping icing and a tip #1. This last detail adds beautiful texture!

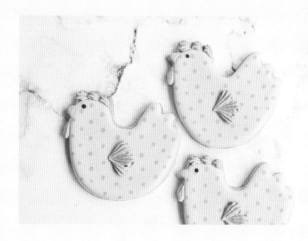

Dottie Spring Chicken Cookie

Only a chicken with silly icing colors and polka dots would lay colorful Easter eggs. These whimsical cookies will leave your guests clucking for more!

Yield: *6 cookies*

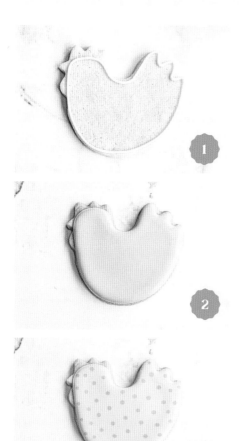

OUTLINE THE COOKIES

Step 1: Outline the body of the chicken with pastel golden yellow piping icing and a tip #2. Be sure to leave room at the top for the chicken comb and a little room on the front for the beak and wattle.

FLOOD THE COOKIES

We are going to use a wet-on-wet technique to add the polka dots to the body of the chicken!

Step 2: Flood in the body of the chicken with the pastel golden yellow.

Step 3: Immediately, while the base layer is still wet, use the dark golden yellow flood icing (don't use piping icing; it won't work!), and add drops of icing to the base layer. Work quickly so the icing doesn't set up too fast. The darker golden yellow drops should melt into the background, creating a flat layer of icing. If the dots still look raised, pick up the cookie and give it a good shimmy to settle the icing flat!

Stop and dry the iced cookies in front of a fan for 1 hour before adding the details.

ADD THE DETAILS

Step 4: Use the dark bakers rose piping icing and the star tip #13 to pipe the wing. The wing is three large piped teardrops. With strong hand pressure, pipe the center teardrop of icing. Squeeze hard and then ease off the pressure as you drag out the tail. Then pipe two more teardrops on either side, matching up the tails with the center teardrop. This creates a quick wing detail that has lots of texture from the star tip!

Still using the dark bakers rose piping icing and the star tip #13, pipe three small teardrops along the top of the head creating the chicken's comb.

Step 5: Switch tips on the dark bakers rose piping icing to a tip #2 and pipe a teardrop for the chicken's wattle.

Step 6: Using the dark golden yellow flood icing, add the beak. Since this icing is thinner, use the scribe or a toothpick to tap the icing into place to create the beak's shape.

Using black piping icing and a tip #1, add a small dot for the eye.

Hippity Hoppity Bunny Cookie

The farmhouse Easter platter would not be complete without a bunny cookie! With the wet-on-wet gingham pattern, these bunnies bring the farmhouse vibes but keep decorating time at a minimum.

Yield: *6 cookies*

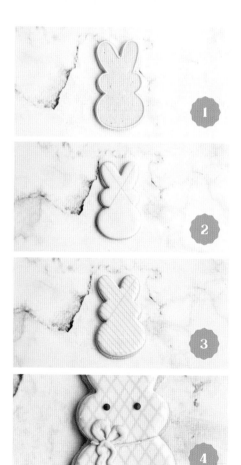

OUTLINE THE COOKIES

Step 1: Outline the bunny using pastel bakers rose piping icing and a tip #2. This outline is intentionally a different color from the flood because it is meant to be seen.

FLOOD THE COOKIES

We are going to use a gingham variation of wet-on-wet stripes for this cute bunny cookie. (See page 23 for tips on creating wet-on-wet stripes.)

Step 2: Flood in the bunny using the white flood icing. Take care not to overflow the base white icing. We will be adding more icing to the cookie since this is a wet-on-wet technique. While that base layer is still wet, use the pastel bakers rose to start the gingham pattern. To help keep spacing consistent, it is helpful to start with adding a pink "x" to the cookie. Start the lines in the middle of the bunny's ear to the bottom of the head.

Step 3: Then add lines of flood icing diagonally across the cookie. The pink lines should melt into the white, creating a flat layer of icing. After adding lines left to right, alternate the lines and go right to left. The result should be a simple gingham pattern.

Stop and dry the iced cookies in front of a fan for 1 hour.

ADD THE DETAILS

Step 4: Add a pastel turquoise bow at the neckline of the bunny. Vary the hand pressure to create thin and thick areas on the bow. Squeeze hard to thicken the line, and ease off the hand pressure to create thin delicate lines. Add the eyes using the black piping icing and a tip #2.

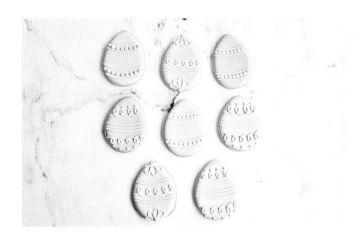

Loops and Swirls Easter Eggs

I love all the pretty pastel icing colors of this set, and they really shine on these colorful and delicious Easter Egg cookies! Not only are they the most fun to decorate, but the eggs are also the easiest cookie on the platter. I made these cookies last, using up the leftover icing I had from the previous designs on the platter.

Yield: *8 cookies*

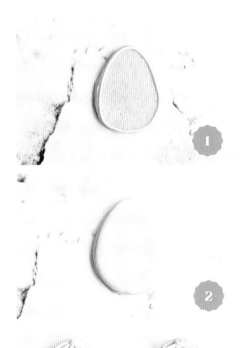

OUTLINE THE COOKIES

Step 1: Outline the cookie with piping icing in the color of your choice and a tip #2. You might want to vary colors from egg to egg to have an assortment of colors on the platter.

FLOOD THE COOKIES

Step 2: Flood in the egg with flood icing in the color of your choice—the same as your outline.

Stop and dry the iced cookies in front of a fan for 1 hour before adding the details.

ADD THE DETAILS

Step 3: Using a tip #2 and the icing color of your choice, have fun piping loops, dots, stripes, swirls and lines to create these colorful eggs. Use a combination of these techniques and make each egg unique! Use the piping practice sheet on page 146 to perfect your skills.

Mother's Day Gardening

Our family always plants flowers on Mother's Day; it's a tradition. The joy of gardening and the joy of cookie deocrating certainly have a lot in common. Getting busy with your hands and getting a little messy, all with a beautiful result. The feature cookie of this platter is the seed packet, but the rubber boot accent cookie is so chubby and fun, it might steal the show! The other accent cookies are the mini flower and the watering can cookies. You can make these cookies as a set or just pick one design to keep things simple. Just keep in mind that the feature Flower Seed Packet Cookie has more steps and is the most time-consuming to create.

Yield: *18 full-size cookies total (6 seed packets, 6 watering cans and 6 rubber boot cookies) and 11 mini flower cookies*

TO MAKE THIS PLATTER YOU'LL NEED

- 1 batch Foolproof Cut-Out Cookie dough (page 12)
- 1 batch Royal Icing (page 14)
- Icing colors (I used Chefmaster, see "Colors by the Ounce")

CUTTERS

- Rectangle cookie cutter
- Rubber Boot cookie cutter
- Watering Can cookie cutter
- Mini 2" (5-cm) Flower cookie cutter

TIPS AND TOOLS

- 5 tips #2
- 3 Wilton tips #129 (drop flower tip)
- 1 Ateco tip #44
- 5 couplers
- 10 icing bags (5 icing bags for piping and 5 bags, or bottles, for flooding)
- Parchment paper
- Cookie sheets
- Toothpick or scribe

STEP 1: PREP THE COOKIES

Use the Foolproof Cut-Out Cookie Recipe on page 12 to bake your cookies, cutting six of each full-size cookie cutter design and eleven of the mini flowers.

STEP 2: MIX THE ICING AND PREP THE COLORS

Use the Royal Icing Recipe on page 14 to mix a single batch of icing (18 to 20 ounces [530 to 600 ml]). Divide the icing into bowls and make the five icing colors according to the guide below.

STEP 3: ADJUST THE ICING CONSISTENCY

When you're ready to decorate, adjust the consistency of the different icing colors to create stiff piping icing, regular piping icing and flooding icing according to the amounts below. For a refresher on making icing consistencies, see page 16. Once the colors are ready, prep them into piping bags, referring to the individual decorating tutorials for details.

COLORS BY THE OUNCE

- Pastel Fuchsia Icing: 5 oz (150 ml) (1 oz [30 ml] for *stiff* pipe and 4 oz [120 ml] for flood)
- Mint Green Icing: 4 oz (120 ml) (1 oz [30 ml] for pipe and 3 oz [90 ml] for flood)
- Lemon Yellow Icing: 5 oz (150 ml) (1 oz [30 ml] for *stiff* pipe and 4 oz [120 ml] for flood)
- Violet Icing: 3 oz (90 ml) (1 oz [30 ml] for *stiff* pipe and 2 oz [60 ml] for flood)
- White Icing: 3 oz (90 ml) (1 oz [30 ml] for pipe and 2 oz [60 ml] for flood)

Now that your cookies and icing are prepped, it's time to decorate! Use the instructions for each individual cookie to help decorate this gardening cookie platter!

Flower Seed Packet Cookie

It all starts with a seed, or in this case, a bit of flour and sugar! I like to make this cookie and coordinate the colors of the flowers on the packet with the mini flowers in the set.

Yield: *6 cookies*

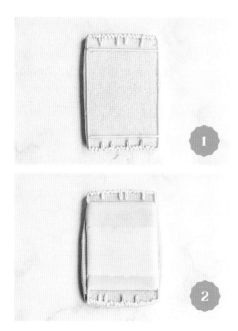

OUTLINE THE COOKIES

Step 1: First outline the sides of the seed packet using mint green piping icing and a tip #2. Add an interesting perforated edge to the top and bottom of the packet. Use a quick wiggle or zigzag motion to pipe that texture. Then add two more horizontal lines in the packet to finish the outline on this cookie.

FLOOD THE COOKIES

Step 2: Flood the main section of the packet using both mint green and white flood icing. Start with the mint green, filling in the top and bottom area. Notice, the top section is wider, about 1 inch (2.5 cm), to allow room to pipe the word "SEEDS" later on. The bottom section is about ½ inch (1.3 cm). While the green icing is still wet, flood the center section with white flood icing, bumping the white against the mint green. This will create a flat surface when the icing is dry.

Stop and dry the iced cookies in front of a fan for 1 to 2 hours before flooding the next section. It's helpful to work in groups of cookies. While one tray is drying, move on to the next tray. See my notes on decorating in an assembly line on page 25.

Step 3: Flood the top and bottom portions of the packet using white flood icing. Wiggle the icing into the nooks and crannies of the piped green outline, but don't cover it. It helps to use a light squeeze on the bag so that you don't add too much icing to this section. The goal is to have the green outline visible so that the perforated detail is accentuated.

Stop and dry the iced cookies in front of a fan for 30 minutes before adding the details.

ADD THE DETAILS

Step 4: It's time to add the cute drop flowers. There are two good options for making these flowers and using them on the cookie. You can pipe these directly on the surface of the cookie, or you could also make these ahead of time if you don't want to worry about poking your icing tip into the surface of the icing.

You'll need a tip #129 (or #224 or #225) for your yellow, violet and fuchsia piping icing. To create the drop flower, use stiff icing. If it is too thin, the flowers will look like blobs and won't hold their shape. Keep the icing bag upright, at a 90-degree angle to the surface of the cookie. As you start to squeeze the icing, start to twist your wrist in a clockwise motion and watch the petals of the flower spread and twist out. Lift the tip straight up. Finish off the flower with a dot of white piping icing and from a tip #2. Add three flowers, using yellow, fuchsia and violet stiff icing.

If you are piping directly on the surface of the cookie, make sure you allow a little extra drying time with the base icing on the cookie so that you can pipe the flowers on top without denting the icing (2 hours instead of 1 hour).

If you are making these flowers in advance, tape a piece of parchment to a cookie sheet. Then make the flowers on the surface of the parchment. Allow the flowers to dry 6 hours before removing them. They will be like a little royal icing candy. You can add a dot of royal icing as "glue" on the back and pop the flower onto the cookie surface. Make extra flowers and store in an airtight container for a future projects. I love having these little flower accents on hand.

Step 5: Add the stems and leaves to the flowers using the mint green piping icing and a tip #2. Squeeze a teardrop of icing to create each leaf. Use a strong squeeze and then ease off the hand pressure as you pull the tip of the leaf out. Pipe the letters for "SEEDS" at the top using violet piping icing and a tip #2. With only five letters, be confident that you can pipe this freehand. Practice piping the letters on a piece of parchment (practicing the spacing size of the letters) before jumping to the cookie surface.

Finish the cookie by piping a line of pastel fuchsia using a tip #2 along the top and bottom sections of the packet.

Blooming Rubber Boot Cookie

Rubber boots come in all colors and patterns! To make this cookie, we are going to take wet-on-wet polka dots to the next level and create a cute daisy pattern. A simple buckle detail makes this a fun and easy cookie!

Yield: *6 cookies*

OUTLINE THE COOKIES

Step 1: Outline the yellow section on the boot with yellow piping icing and a tip #2. Then add the violet section at the top with piping icing and a tip #2. Use white piping icing and a tip #2 to create the sole on the boot. Pipe a scalloped line at the base to make it look like a boot tread.

FLOOD THE COOKIES

Step 2: Flood the main section of the boot with yellow icing. While that base layer of icing is still wet, add the wet-on-wet daisies. This is similar to adding wet-on-wet polka dots (see the tips for wet-on-wet polka dots on page 23).

First, add the violet dots (the center of the flower). Minimize your work by spacing out the dots. I added three dots across the top of the boot and four dots down the center of the boot. This spacing will allow room for the pink petals on the flowers.

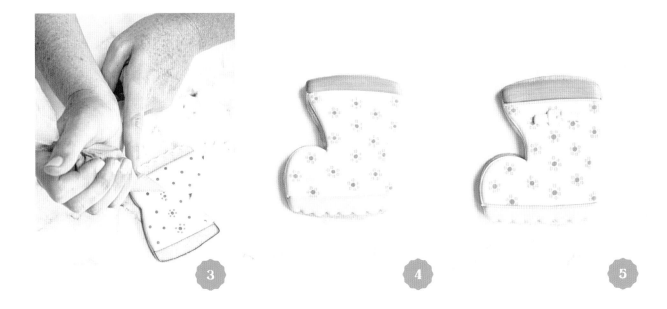

Step 3: Once all the violet dots are added to the cookie, it's time to add the pink petals. These are just more dots. Add six fuchsia dots around each violet dot to make the flower.

With this many dots being added to the cookie, be sure to work quickly so the yellow base icing doesn't set before all the dots are added. If any dots are raised, shimmy the cookie to settle the icing.

Stop and dry the iced cookies in front of a fan for 1 hour before flooding the next sections.

Step 4: Flood the top of the boot with purple flood icing. Flood the bottom of the boot with white flood icing.

Stop and dry the iced cookies in front of a fan for 30 minutes before adding the details.

ADD THE DETAILS

Step 5: Add a line between the seams of the top and bottom of the boot using fuchsia piping icing and a tip #2. Add the buckle using yellow piping icing and the tip #44. Keep the tip horizontal and flat to pipe a wide stripe of icing. Then add the buckle using white piping icing and a tip #2.

Daisy Watering Can Cookie

Gardens need lots of love, sunshine and water! This cute Watering Can cookie is essential to making this gardening set complete.

Yield: *6 cookies*

OUTLINE THE COOKIES

Step 1: Outline the watering can using fuchsia piping icing and a tip #2. I pipe the main body of the watering can first and then add the handle section and the base. Circle out a little area for the spout. We will flood those areas separately to create natural definition lines.

FLOOD THE COOKIES

Step 2: Flood the main body of the watering can with fuchsia flood icing.

Stop and dry the iced cookies in front of a fan for 1 hour before flooding the next sections.

Step 3: Flood the handle and the base using fuchsia flood icing. Flood the spout in white and add some wet-on-wet violet dots. This isn't a big icing area, so keep these dots small. Make sure the opening trimmed on the violet flood bag is small. You could also build this bag with a tip #1 to make sure you have a small opening. Review the tips on page 23 for a refresher on how to create wet-on-wet polka dots.

Stop and dry the iced cookies in front of a fan for 30 minutes before adding the details.

ADD THE DETAILS

Step 4: Pipe fuchsia detail lines around the spout and the top of the watering can using piping icing and a tip #2. Add accent lines on the can using white and mint green piping icing and a tip #2. Add the daisy in the center. Pipe the petals first using a tip #2, making six small teardrops of white piping icing that meet in the middle, then add a yellow center.

Itty Bitty
Flower Cookie

Bite-size cookies are always a hit! Even better, mini cookies are often simpler and quicker to decorate, making them the perfect addition to this platter.

Yield: *11 mini cookies*

There are no outlines on this cookie! Because it is a mini, we are going to jump right to the flooding.

FLOOD THE COOKIES

Step 1: Flood in alternating petals on the flower using any icing color and flood icing. Each petal is a teardrop shape of icing. Start the wide end of the teardrop at the edge of the cookie (not too close to the edge—you don't want it to flow off the side). Squeeze the icing using strong hand pressure, tapering off as you pull out the teardrop shape into the center of the cookie.

Stop and dry the iced cookies in front of a fan for 30 minutes before flooding the next sections.

Step 2: Flood in the remaining petals using flood icing. Don't worry if the petals don't meet in the middle; we will add a center to the flower that will cover up that area.

Stop and dry the iced cookies in front of a fan for 30 minutes before adding the details.

ADD THE DETAILS

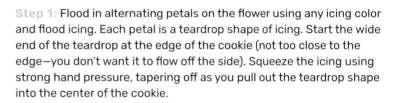

Step 3: Add the center of the flower using white piping icing and a tip #2. Then add beads of icing around the center of the flower in an accent icing color.

Hello Summer Cookies

Long days and outdoor gatherings make summer days the best! Whether you're
at the beach or a cookout, bringing cookies will always be welcome.

In this chapter, kick off the summer by honoring dads and their love for grilling with
cookies full of personality (page 101). Then celebrate the USA, and enjoy the ease
of the Red, White & Boom! icing palette (page 109). Get the summer vibes going
with the Fun in the Sun cookie set (page 115) and learn how to make
some beach essentials.

Father's Day Grilling

Fire up the barbie (and your oven); it's cookie time! If the dad in your life is the king of the grill, he'll think these cookies are flippin' awesome!

The feature cookie of this platter is the cheeseburger cookie. The accent cookies are the grill, hot dog and ketchup and mustard. You can make these cookies as a set or just pick one design to keep things simple. Just keep in mind that the feature cheeseburger cookie has more steps and is the most time-consuming to create.

Yield: *25 cookies total (7 cheeseburgers, 6 grills, 6 hot dogs, 3 ketchup bottles and 3 mustard bottles)*

TO MAKE THIS PLATTER YOU'LL NEED

- 1 batch Foolproof Cut-Out Cookie dough (page 12)
- 1 batch Royal Icing (page 14)
- Icing colors (I used Chefmaster, see "Colors by the Ounce")

CUTTERS

- Hamburger cookie cutter
- Grill cookie cutter
- Hot Dog cookie cutter
- Crayon cookie cutter (used for both the Ketchup and Mustard)

TIPS AND TOOLS

- 7 tips #2
- 1 tip #3
- 1 tip #1
- 1 Wilton tip #352
- 8 couplers
- 13 icing bags (6 icing bags for piping, 2 bags for 20-second icing and 5 bags, or bottles, for flooding)
- Parchment paper
- Cookie sheets
- Toothpick or scribe
- Crystal Color carnation pink dust, to blush the cheeks
- Food-safe round brush

STEP 1: PREP THE COOKIES

Use the Foolproof Cut-Out Cookie Recipe on page 12 to bake your cookies, cutting seven hamburger shapes, six grill shapes, six of the hot dog shapes and six of the crayon cutter shapes for the ketchup and mustard bottle cookies.

STEP 2: MIX THE ICING AND PREP THE COLORS

Use the Royal Icing Recipe on page 14 to mix a single batch of icing (18 to 20 ounces [530 to 600 ml]). Divide the icing into bowls and make the eight icing colors according to the guide on the following page.

STEP 3: ADJUST THE ICING CONSISTENCY

When you're ready to decorate, adjust the consistency of the different icing colors to create stiff icing, piping icing, 20-second icing and flooding icing according to the amounts on the following page. For a refresher on making icing consistencies, see page 16. Once the colors are ready, prep them into piping bags, referring to the individual decorating tutorials for details.

(Continued)

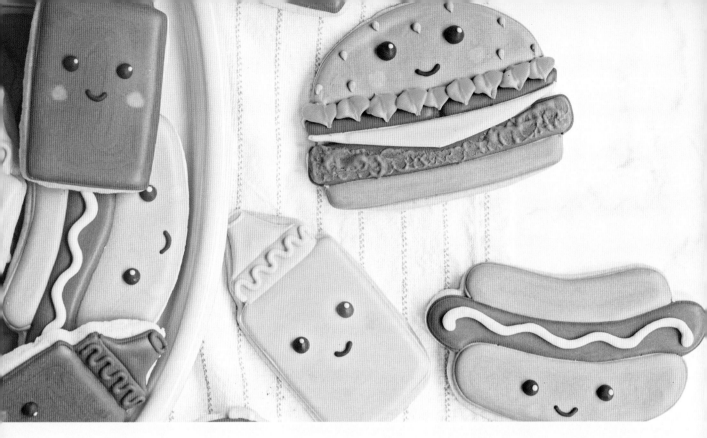

Father's Day Grilling (Continued)

COLORS BY THE OUNCE

- Super Red Icing: 4 oz (120 ml) (1 oz [30 ml] for pipe and 3 oz [90 ml] for flood)
- Golden Yellow Icing: 3 oz (90 ml) (1 oz [30 ml] for pipe and 2 oz [60 ml] for flood)
- Light Brown Icing: 5 oz (150 ml) (1 oz [30 ml] for pipe and 4 oz [120 ml] for flood)
- Dark Brown Icing: 2 oz (60 ml) (1 oz [30 ml] for pipe and 1 oz [30 ml] for flood)
- Reddish Brown Icing (mix equal parts Super Red and Buckeye Brown): 2 oz (60 ml) (1 oz [30 ml] for pipe and 1 oz [30 ml] for flood)
- Black Icing: 2 oz (60 ml) (for 20-second icing only)
- Gray Icing: 1 oz (30 ml) (for 20-second icing only)
- Leaf Green Icing: 1 oz (30 ml) (for *stiff* pipe only)

Now that your cookies and icing are prepped, it's time to decorate! Use the instructions for each individual cookie to help decorate this Father's Day Grilling cookie platter!

Cheeseburger with All the Fixings Cookie

Dads love cookies and this cheeseburger will make their mouths water! This cookie has lots of fun textures, making it a feast for the eyes and mouth.

Yield: *7 cookies*

OUTLINE THE COOKIES

Step 1: Start by outlining the top and bottom buns using light brown piping icing and a tip #2. Then outline the burger patty using the dark brown piping icing and a tip #2. Outline two small rectangles for tomatoes using the red piping icing and a tip #2.

FLOOD THE COOKIES

Step 2: Fill in the top bun using light brown flood icing. Flood the tomatoes using the red flood icing. Then flood in the burger patty using dark brown flood icing.

Stop and dry the iced cookies in front of a fan for 1 hour before flooding the next section. It's helpful to work in groups of cookies. While one tray is drying move onto the next tray. See my notes on decorating in an assembly line on page 25.

Step 3: Outline the cheese triangle using the golden yellow piping icing and a tip #2. Pipe the line against the bottom of the tomatoes and overlap it over the burger.

(Continued)

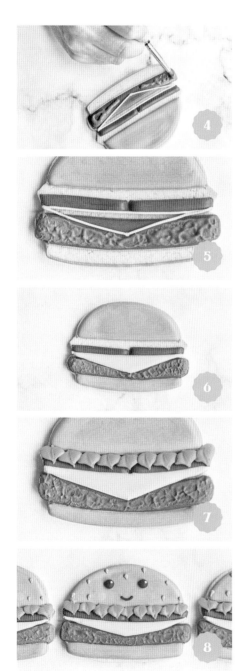

Step 4: Now create the texture on the burger. Squeeze a few dots of the dark brown flood on the surface of the burger patty. Then use a round food-safe brush and dab the icing.

Step 5: Keep dabbing until you achieve an even texture on the surface of the burger.

Step 6: Fill in the cheese using the golden yellow flood icing. Then fill in the bottom bun using light brown flood icing.

Step 7: Add the lettuce using the green stiff piping icing and the tip #352. It's helpful for the icing to be stiff so that the icing stays in a leaf shape. Wiggle the tip between the top bun and tomatoes and give a strong squeeze to create each little leaf/lettuce and fill in that gap.

Stop and dry the iced cookies in front of a fan for 30 minutes before adding the piped details.

ADD THE DETAILS

Step 8: Add the face using the black 20-second icing and a tip #2. Add the eyes first, spacing them out, and then add a teeny dot of gray with the tip #1 for the catchlight. Pipe a small smile centered between the eyes. Then use the carnation pink edible dust to blush the cheeks. Use a small round brush and gently brush in circles to create the rosy cheeks. Add seeds to the bun using light brown piping icing and a tip #2.

King of the Grill Cookie

Whether your dad uses gas or charcoal, this grill cookie will be welcome at the cookout! Using the 20-second icing on the small icing areas will help this cookie come together quickly.

Yield: *6 cookies*

OUTLINE THE COOKIES

Step 1: Outline the center section of the grill, the lip of the lid and base using gray 20-second icing and a tip #2. Pipe the red lid and base using red piping icing and a tip #2. Add the legs and wheels. Follow the shape of the cookie using black 20-second icing and a tip #2.

FLOOD THE COOKIES

Step 2: Fill in the center section of the grill, the lip of the lid and base using the gray 20-second icing. Fill in the legs using black 20-second icing. Flood in the wheel using black icing. While the black icing is still wet, add a drop of gray icing on the wheel as a wet-on-wet dot.

Stop and dry the iced cookies in front of a fan for 30 minutes before flooding the next sections.

Step 3: Flood in the top and base of the grill using the red flood icing.

Stop and dry the iced cookies in front of a fan for 1 hour before adding the details.

ADD THE DETAILS

Step 4: Use the gray 20-second icing and a tip #2 to add a small square for the vent on the lid of the grill, pipe the handle and add a piped line detail on the lip of the lid. Add 8 mini wet-on-wet dots with black icing to the vent on the grill. Add the face using the black 20-second icing and a tip #2. Add the eyes first, spacing them out. Add a teeny dot of gray with the tip #1 for the catchlight. Pipe a small smile centered between the eyes. Then use the carnation pink edible dust and a small round brush to blush the cheeks.

Hot Diggity Dog Cookie

Hot diggity happy hot dogs! While the details on this cookie are totally approachable, this cookie requires a bit of color mixing. To get the perfect hot dog color, add a few dots of Super Red and Buckeye Brown food gel to get the right shade for your icing.

Yield: *6 cookies*

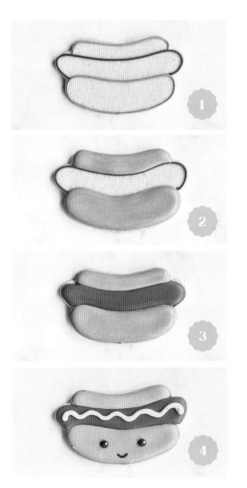

OUTLINE THE COOKIES

Step 1: Outline the bottom bun using light brown piping icing and a tip #2. Then pipe the hot dog section using the red/brown piping icing and a tip #2. Finish off the outlines by piping the top bun using light brown piping icing and a tip #2.

FLOOD THE COOKIES

Step 2: Fill in both buns using the light brown flood icing.

Stop and dry the iced cookies in front of a fan for 1 hour before flooding the next section.

Step 3: Fill in the hot dog using the red/brown flood icing.

Stop and dry the iced cookies in front of a fan for 30 minutes before adding the details.

ADD THE DETAILS

Step 4: Put a tip #3 on the golden yellow piping icing and add a wiggly line for the mustard. Add the face using the black 20-second icing and a tip #2. Add the eyes first, spacing them out. Add a teeny dot of gray with the tip #1 for the catchlight. Pipe a small smile centered between the eyes. Then use the carnation pink edible dust to blush the cheeks. Use a small round brush and gently brush in circles to create the rosy cheeks.

Happy Mustard and Ketchup Cookie

Getting creative with cookie cutters makes decorating super fun! These mustard and ketchup bottles are made using the crayon cookie cutter. It's perfect! See the crayon cookies on page 127.

Yield: *6 cookies*

OUTLINE THE COOKIES

Step 1: Outline the mustard bottle and lid using the golden yellow piping icing and a tip #2.

FLOOD THE COOKIES

Step 2: Fill in the main body of the mustard bottle and the tip using the golden yellow flood icing.

Stop and dry the iced cookies in front of a fan for 1 hour before flooding the next section.

Step 3: Fill in the small section of the lid using the golden yellow flood icing.

Stop and dry the iced cookies in front of a fan for 30 minutes before adding the details.

ADD THE DETAILS

Step 4: Add a wiggly line on the lid using golden yellow piping icing and a tip #2. Add the face using the black 20-second icing and a tip #2. Add the eyes first. Space them out and add a teeny dot of gray with the tip #1 for the catchlight. Pipe a small smile centered between the eyes. Then use the carnation pink edible dust to blush the cheeks. Use a small round brush and gently brush in circles to create the rosy cheeks.

Repeat these same steps using the red piping icing and red flood icing to create the happy ketchup cookie.

Red, White & Boom!

Red, white and blue forever! Royal icing won't melt at those steaming hot July Fourth picnics, making these the perfect treat for the dessert table! The feature cookie of this platter is the USA cookie. The accent cookies are the firecrackers and the popsicles. You can make these cookies as a set or just pick one design to keep things simple. Just keep in mind that the feature USA cookie has more steps and is the most time-consuming to create. The USA cookie is the only one in the book that employs an airbrush machine. This is a great decorating tool for quickly adding beautiful backgrounds, but as an alternative, try a can of the silver Wilton Color Mist. While these designs are specific to the United States, many countries celebrate an independence day. Using colors and images from your national flag, it would be fun to tweak these cookie concepts to personalize your celebration. If you can't readily find a cookie cutter in the shape of your country, consider a rectangle to represent a flag design.

Yield: *21 cookies total (7 USA maps, 7 firecrackers and 7 popsicles)*

TO MAKE THIS PLATTER YOU'LL NEED

- 1 batch Foolproof Cut-Out Cookie dough (page 12)
- 1 batch Royal Icing (page 14)
- Icing colors (I used Chefmaster, see "Colors by the Ounce")

CUTTERS

- USA Map cookie cutter
- Firecracker cookie cutter
- Popsicle cookie cutter

TIPS AND TOOLS

- 4 tips #2
- 1 tip #3
- 5 couplers
- 8 icing bags (3 icing bags for piping, 2 bags for 20-second icing and 3 bags, or bottles, for flooding)
- Parchment paper
- Cookie sheets
- Toothpick or scribe
- Stars stencil
- Silver airbrush color (or silver Wilton Color Mist can)
- Stencil genie (optional)
- Airbrush system (optional)

STEP 1: PREP THE COOKIES

Use the Foolproof Cut-Out Cookie Recipe on page 12 to bake your cookies, cutting seven of each cookie cutter design.

STEP 2: MIX THE ICING AND PREP THE COLORS

Use the Royal Icing Recipe on page 14 to mix a single batch of icing (approximately 18 to 20 ounces [530 to 600 ml]). Divide the icing into bowls and make the five icing colors according to the guide below.

STEP 3: ADJUST THE ICING CONSISTENCY

When you're ready to decorate, adjust the consistency of the different icing colors to create piping icing, 20-second icing and flooding icing according to the amounts below. For a refresher on making icing consistencies, see page 16. Once the colors are ready, prep them into piping bags.

COLORS BY THE OUNCE

- Super Red Icing: 4 oz (120 ml) (1 oz [30 ml] for pipe and 3 oz [90 ml] for flood)
- Royal Blue Icing: 4 oz (120 ml) (1 oz [30 ml] for pipe and 3 oz [90 ml] for flood)
- White Icing: 8 oz (240 ml) (1 oz [30 ml] for pipe and 7 oz [210 ml] for flood)
- Lemon Yellow Icing: 1 oz (30 ml) (for 20-second icing only)
- Light Brown Icing: 1 oz (30 ml) (for 20-second icing only)

Now that your cookies and icing are prepped, it's time to decorate! Use the instructions for each individual cookie to help decorate this Red, White & Boom! cookie platter!

Hooray for the USA Cookie

Celebrate the land of liberty with these USA map cookies! This impressive silver star background and puffy letters will have picnickers cheering, "Hooray for the USA!" Independence day celebrations are not unique to the United States. I encourage you to customize this design for international celebrations. In this project, I'm using stars, but if celebrating Canada I would use a maple leaf. Have fun planning the background and design to celebrate your heritage!

Yield: *7 cookies*

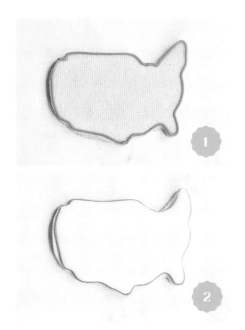

OUTLINE THE COOKIES

Step 1: Outline the shape of the USA cookic using royal blue piping icing and a tip #2. I like to see the accent of the blue outline peeking out from the white icing base.

FLOOD THE COOKIES

Step 2: Fill in the entire cookie generously using the white flood icing.

Stop and dry the iced cookies in front of a fan for 1 hour before stenciling. It's helpful to work in groups of cookies. While one tray is drying, move onto the next tray. See my notes on decorating in an assembly line on page 25.

Step 3: Stenciling on cookies is a great way to add a new color, a pattern or a beautiful background. You can use an airbrush machine like I did, but there are also several food color spray can options, like Wilton's Color Mist, that are affordable and work really well.

When stenciling on cookies, it's very helpful to use a stencil frame called a Stencil Genie. It keeps the stencil in place and prevents it from blowing or shifting during stenciling. If you don't have a Stencil Genie, no worries. You can simply rest your wrist on the tabletop to hold the stencil in place while spraying the color with your other hand.

Place the stencil over the icing. The stencil should be sitting on the surface of the icing, otherwise color can sneak up under the stencil and create a blurry image. Apply the color using the airbrush machine or can. Aim the color straight down at the cookie for the best image. Don't blow color across the stencil because the color might sneak under the stencil. Apply color lightly to start. If too much is added, the color can run or form beads of color on the surface of the icing. More color can always be added if needed, so start with a light application. Once the desired coverage is reached, gently lift back the stencil being careful not to smudge the image.

Plan for a tester cookie or two, to allow for some practice using spray and stencils.

Stop and dry the airbrushed area in front of a fan for 20 minutes before adding the piped details.

ADD THE DETAILS

Step 4: Pipe the letters U-S-A using blue and red piping icing and a tip #2. Pipe the red "S" first, centering it on the cookie. Add a double line to thicken the letters. Then add the "U" and "A" using the blue piping icing and a tip #2. Again, add a double line to thicken the letters.

Step 5: Fill in the small sections of the letters using the blue and red flood icing. Put the cookies in front of a fan for 15 minutes to quick-dry those little icing areas.

Step 6: Add loops, lines and dots to create little fireworks on the cookie using red piping icing and a tip #2.

Red, White & Boom Firecracker Cookie

These firecracker cookies are guaranteed oohs and aahs over your cookie platter! The 20-second icing consistency plays an essential role on this cookie (refer to page 16 for a review of icing consistencies). When the consistency is just right, not too thick and not too thin, the sparks have a smooth puffiness that look so cool.

Yield: *7 cookies*

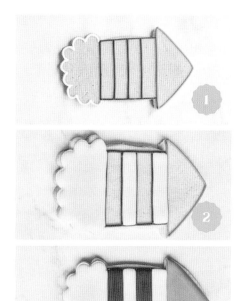

OUTLINE THE COOKIES

Step 1: Outline the top of the firecracker using royal blue piping icing and a tip #2. Outline the body of the firecracker using red piping icing and a tip #2. Add three horizontal lines to section off the stripes, then outline the bottom section using white piping icing and a tip #2.

FLOOD THE COOKIES

Step 2: Fill in the first and third stripes using the white flood icing. Then fill in the bottom section in white.

Stop and dry the iced cookies in front of a fan for 1 hour before flooding the next sections.

Step 3: Flood in the top using the blue flood icing. Fill in the remaining stripes using red flood icing.

Stop and dry the iced cookies in front of a fan for 1 hour before adding the details.

ADD THE DETAILS

Step 4: Use the brown 20-second icing and a tip #2 to pipe the fuse. Add the "sparks" using yellow 20-second icing and the tip #3. Start at the end of the spark, near the bottom of the cookie. Use a strong squeeze at first and then ease into a light squeeze to create a tapered look to each spark. Then add five curved lines with white piping icing and a tip #2 to add a fun detail to the top of the firecracker.

Patriotic Popsicle Cookie

Take an ordinary summer cookie shape, like a popsicle, and make it super festive with red, white and blue icing colors. Pipe dots and lines to give off the stars and stripes vibe!

Yield: *7 cookies*

OUTLINE THE COOKIES

Step 1: Outline the top of the pop with royal blue piping icing and a tip #2. This section is about one-third of the cookie. Then outline the base of the pop using red piping icing and a tip #2.

FLOOD THE COOKIES

Step 2: Fill in the top using blue flood icing. Outline the pop stick using brown 20-second icing and a tip #2. Then fill in the stick with the same 20-second icing.

Stop and dry the iced cookies in front of a fan for 1 hour before flooding the next section.

Step 3: Fill in the bottom of the pop using red flood icing.

Stop and dry the iced cookies in front of a fan for 1 hour before adding the details.

ADD THE DETAILS

Step 4: Add several rows of dots on the top. Use a 3-2-3-2 pattern to keep the spacing even. Then add the stipes using the white and blue piping icing and a tip #2.

Fun in the Sun

Sun hat. Check! Swimsuit. Check! Sandals. Check! Cookies. Check! A perfect summer day is not complete without the perfect summer cookie platter.

The feature cookie of this platter is the sandal. The accent cookies are the sun hats and swimsuits. You can make these cookies as a set or just pick one design to keep things simple. Just keep in mind that the feature sandal cookie has more steps and is the most time-consuming to create.

Yield: *21 cookies total (7 sandals, 7 swimsuits and 7 sun hats)*

TO MAKE THIS PLATTER YOU'LL NEED

- 1 batch Foolproof Cut-Out Cookie dough (page 12)
- 1 batch Royal Icing (page 14)
- Icing colors (I used Chefmaster, see "Colors by the Ounce")

CUTTERS

- Flip-Flop cookie cutter
- Swimming Suit One Piece cookie cutter
- Bonnet cookie cutter

TIPS AND TOOLS

- 6 tips #2
- 2 tips #1
- 1 tip #3
- 1 Wilton tip #301
- 6 couplers
- 12 icing bags (6 icing bags for piping and 6 bags, or bottles, for flooding)
- Parchment paper
- Cookie sheets
- Toothpick or scribe
- Yellow food marker
- Sandal template (page 145)

STEP 1: PREP THE COOKIES

Use the Foolproof Cut-Out Cookie Recipe on page 12 to bake your cookies, cutting seven of each cookie cutter design.

STEP 2: MIX THE ICING AND PREP THE COLORS

Use the Royal Icing Recipe on page 14 to mix a single batch of icing (18 to 20 ounces [530 to 600 ml]). Divide the icing into bowls and make the six icing colors according to the guide below.

STEP 3: ADJUST THE ICING CONSISTENCY

When you're ready to decorate, adjust the consistency of the different icing colors to create piping icing and flooding icing according to the amounts below. For a refresher on making icing consistencies, see page 16. Once the colors are ready, prep them into piping bags, referring to the individual decorating tutorials for details.

COLORS BY THE OUNCE

- Light Brown Icing: 5 oz (150 ml) (1 oz [30 ml] for pipe and 4 oz [120 ml] for flood)
- Teal Icing: 3 oz (90 ml) (1 oz [30 ml] for pipe and 2 oz [60 ml] for flood)
- Lemon Yellow Icing: 3 oz (90 ml) (1 oz [30 ml] for pipe and 2 oz [60 ml] for flood)
- Georgia Peach Icing: 4 oz (120 ml) (1 oz [30 ml] for pipe and 3 oz [90 ml] for flood)
- White Icing: 3 oz (90 ml) (1 oz [30 ml] for pipe and 2 oz [60 ml] for flood)
- Black Icing: 2 oz (60 ml) (1 oz [30 ml] for pipe and 1 oz [30 ml] for flood)

Now that your cookies and icing are prepped, it's time to decorate! Use the instructions for each individual cookie to help decorate this Fun in the Sun cookie platter!

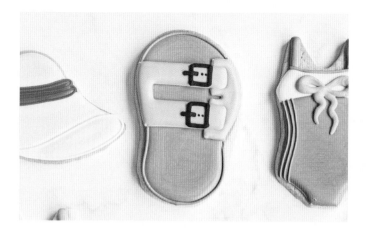

Laid-Back Leather Sandal Cookie

Everyone's favorite leather sandal is now a really cute cookie! Precision is key to successfully creating this cookie, so check out the cookie template for this sandal on page 145.

Yield: *7 cookies*

OUTLINE THE COOKIES

Step 1: Outline the base of the sandal using light brown piping icing and a tip #2.

FLOOD THE COOKIES

Step 2: Flood the entire cookie using the light brown flood icing.

Stop and dry the iced cookies in front of a fan for at least 3 hours before adding the next layer of icing. The dry time is important if you're using a food marker to trace the template onto the light brown icing. If you proceed too soon, the tip of the marker could poke through the surface of the light brown icing. And remember, it's helpful to work in groups of cookies. While one tray is drying, move onto the next tray. See my notes on decorating in an assembly line on page 25.

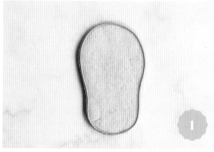

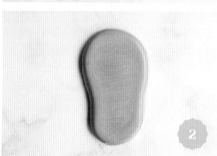

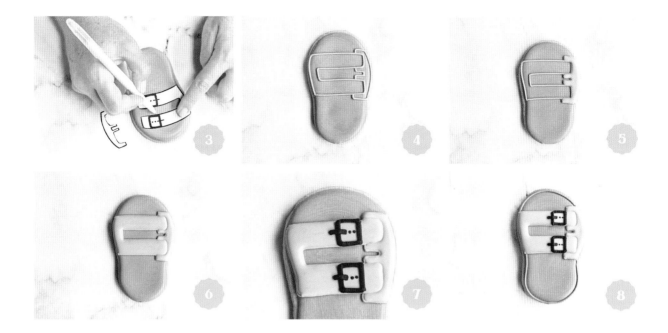

OUTLINE THE LEATHER STRAPS

Step 3: Cut out the leather strap from the template on page 145. Use a light-colored food-safe marker, like yellow, to trace around the edges of the template onto the cookie.

Step 4: Using the traced yellow lines as a guide, pipe the strap outline using teal piping icing and a tip #2.

FLOOD THE LEATHER STRAPS

Step 5: Flood in the small, right section of the leather strap using teal flood icing.

Stop and dry the iced cookies in front of a fan for 30 minutes before flooding the next section.

Step 6: Flood in the left section, bumping the flood icing up and over the first section to give the illusion that these straps are on top.

Stop and dry the iced cookies in front of a fan for 30 minutes before adding the details.

ADD THE DETAILS

Step 7: Use the black piping icing and the tip #301 (a small flat tip) to pipe a square for the buckle. Add the prong, a short line, also using the tip #301. Then switch the tip on the black to a tip #1 and add the two holes.

Step 8: Outline the base of the sandal using light brown piping icing and a tip #2.

Summer Vibes Swimsuit Cookie

This swimsuit cookie can be made in all three bright colors to get all the summer vibes in your platter. This example features the Georgia peach gel color—a perfect shade for summer!

Yield: *7 cookies*

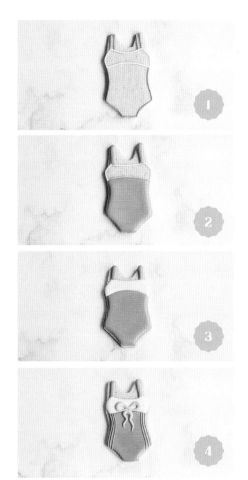

OUTLINE THE COOKIES

Step 1: Outline the top of the swimsuit using white piping icing and a tip #2. Add the straps using peach piping icing and a tip #2. Then outline the body of the suit using peach piping icing and a tip #2.

FLOOD THE COOKIES

Step 2: Flood the straps and body of the suit using the peach flood icing.

Stop and dry the iced cookies in front of a fan for 1 hour before flooding the next section.

Step 3: Flood the top of the bathing suit using white flood icing.

Stop and dry the iced cookies in front of a fan for 30 minutes before adding the details.

ADD THE DETAILS

Step 4: Using peach piping icing and a tip #1, pipe the stripes along the side of the suit. Add the bow to the top of the suit using the #3 tip on the teal piping bag. First pipe the loops on the bow. Use a stronger squeeze where the loops are thicker. Ease off the hand pressure to create the thinner areas on the bow at the center. Then add the two ribbons hanging down. Start with a strong squeeze and then ease the hand pressure to create the tapered look.

Here Comes the Sun Hat Cookie

The playful yellow and white stripes of this sun hat make it a perfect accent to the swimming suit and sandals cookie ensemble. But this sun hat would also be a great addition to the gardening cookie set on page 91!

Yield: *7 cookies*

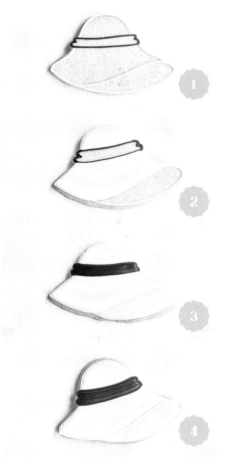

OUTLINE THE COOKIES

Step 1: Start the outline by using black piping icing and a tip #2 to pipe the ribbon. Then, to give the hat a bit of dimension, use the yellow piping icing and tip #2 to pipe the brim. Start the outline in the bottom left and bring the outline up around in a loop shape to create the brim. Finish off the outlines on the top and sides of the hat using the yellow piping icing and a tip #2.

FLOOD THE COOKIES

Step 2: Flood the main section of the hat using white and yellow flood icing. Flood the white stripes first and the add the yellow. Bump the stripes of flood against each other to create a flat icing surface.

Stop and dry the iced cookies in front of a fan for 1 hour before flooding the next sections.

Step 3: Flood the ribbon using black flood icing. Finish the section under the brim using yellow flood icing.

Stop and dry the iced cookies in front of a fan for 30 minutes before adding the details.

ADD THE DETAILS

Step 4: Outline the ribbon section and pipe two lines inside for texture using black icing and a tip #1. Then add a piped line across the brim using yellow piping icing and a tip #2.

Fall Gatherings

When the leaves start to change and the weather turns cool, it's time to welcome the new season with fall cookies!

In this chapter, get a little nerdy with your cookies with the Back to School cookie set (page 123). Then learn how to make treats, not tricks, for Halloween (page 129). Be sure to bring the sprinkles! And finally, celebrate the season of gratitude with a Thanksgiving platter (page 137) that will delight the guests at your Thanksgiving table.

Back to School

Earn some serious extra credit points with these Back to School cookies! They make a delicious gift for teachers, students, bus drivers and staff any time during the school year. The feature cookie of this platter is the Nerdy Apple Cookie. The accent cookies are the pencil and crayon cookies. You can make these cookies as a set or just pick one design to keep things simple.

Yield: *21 cookies total (7 apples, 7 pencils and 7 crayons)*

TO MAKE THIS PLATTER YOU'LL NEED

- 1 batch Foolproof Cut-Out Cookie dough (page 12)
- 2 batches Royal Icing (page 14)
- Icing colors (I used Chefmaster, see "Colors by the Ounce")

CUTTERS

- Cute Apple cookie cutter
- Chunky Pencil cookie cutter
- Crayon cookie cutter (used also for the ketchup and mustard on page 107)

TIPS AND TOOLS

- 8 tips #2
- 1 tip #3
- 1 Wilton tip #67
- 9 couplers, plus an extra optional coupler for tracing the glasses on the apple
- 17 icing bags (9 icing bags for piping and 8 bags, or bottles, for flooding)
- Parchment paper
- Cookie sheets
- Toothpick or scribe
- Yellow food marker (optional)

STEP 1: PREP THE COOKIES

Use the Foolproof Cut-Out Cookie Recipe on page 12 to bake your cookies, cutting seven of each cookie cutter design.

STEP 2: MIX THE ICING AND PREP THE COLORS

Use the Royal Icing Recipe on page 14 to mix a *double* batch of icing (36 to 40 ounces [1 to 1.2 L]). Because this set features nine icing colors, it will be helpful to make extra icing to allow for a little wiggle room. See my tips for storing icing on page 20. Divide the icing into bowls and make the nine icing colors according to the guide below.

STEP 3: ADJUST THE ICING CONSISTENCY

When you're ready to decorate, adjust the consistency of the different icing colors to create stiff icing, piping icing and flooding icing (see page 16). Once the colors are ready, prep them into piping bags.

COLORS BY THE OUNCE

- Super Red Icing: 5 oz (150 ml) (1 oz [30 ml] for pipe and 4 oz [120 ml] for flood)
- Lemon Yellow Icing: 4 oz (120 ml) (1 oz [30 ml] for pipe and 3 oz [90 ml] for flood)
- Light Brown Icing: 3 oz (90 ml) (1 oz [30 ml] for pipe and 2 oz [60 ml] for flood)
- Pastel Pink Icing: 2 oz (60 ml) (1 oz [30 ml] for pipe and 1 oz [30 ml] for flood)
- Sky Blue Icing: 5 oz (150 ml) (1 oz [30 ml] for pipe and 4 oz [120 ml] for flood)
- Black Icing: 2 oz (60 ml) (1 oz [30 ml] for pipe and 1 oz [30 ml] for flood)
- Gray Icing: 2 oz (60 ml) (1 oz [30 ml] for pipe and 1 oz [30 ml] for flood)
- Leaf Green Icing: 1 oz (30 ml) (for *stiff* pipe only)
- White Icing: 2 oz (60 ml) (1 oz [30 ml] for pipe and 1 oz [30 ml] for flood)

Now that your cookies and icing are prepped, it's time to decorate! Use the instructions for each individual cookie to help decorate this Back to School cookie platter!

Nerdy Apple Cookie

Watch this cookie come to life as you create the detailed eyes of the apple. This requires a little extra work, but it will be worth it! This whimsical apple design is not complete without the chunky green leaf created using the tip #67.

Yield: *7 cookies*

TRACE THE GLASSES

Step 1: This first step is optional, but it doesn't take much time and sets this cookie up for success. Using a yellow food-safe marker and a coupler, trace two circles for the eyes onto the cookie.

OUTLINE THE COOKIES

Step 2: Outline the eyes using white piping icing and a tip #2. Outline the apple using red piping icing and a tip #2. Outline the apple stem using the light brown icing and a tip #2.

FLOOD THE COOKIES

Step 3: Fill the main section of the apple using red flood icing.

Stop and dry the iced cookies in front of a fan for 1 hour before flooding the next section. It's helpful to work in groups of cookies. While one tray is drying, move onto the next tray. See my notes on decorating in an assembly line on page 25.

The next four steps use a wet-on-wet technique. Use the flood icing to add the layers of the eyes while the base layer of white is still wet. All the icing layers, since they are the same flood icing consistency, will melt down flat into one layer.

Step 4: First, fill in the apple stem using light brown flood icing. Now it is time to create the eyes. Start by flooding in the white of the eyes.

Step 5: While the white is still wet, add the irises using the sky blue flood icing. Don't overflow the eyes! Be careful how much icing you're adding to this small area.

Step 6: Working quickly, add a dot of black flood icing in the center of the sky blue for the pupil.

Step 7: Finish the eye by adding a tiny dot of white flood icing to add the catchlight. This makes the apple's eyes come alive! All the color layers should melt flat, but if the surface is raised, shimmy the cookie side to side to settle the icing.

Stop and dry the iced cookies in front of a fan for 30 minutes before adding the piped details.

ADD THE DETAILS

Step 8: Switch the tip on your black piping icing to the tip #3. Follow the shape of the eye and add the round glasses. Use the same icing and tip to add the nose bridge and the edge of the frames.

Step 9: Add the details to the face. Switch the tip on the black piping icing to a tip #2 and add eyebrows and a side smile. Then add a nose using the red piping icing and a tip #2. Add a swirl to the stem using light brown piping icing and a tip #2. Finish the cookie with a big chunky green leaf using the tip #67. Keep the tip horizontal to the cookie. Give a strong squeeze to start the wide base of the leaf, then ease off the hand pressure as you pull the leaf out, slimming it down to a point at the end.

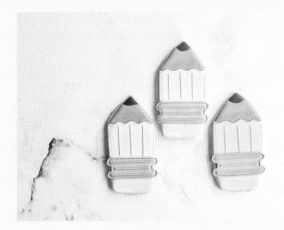

Chunky Yellow Pencil Cookie

Freshly sharpened yellow pencils are a must-have school supply, and so are these chunky pencil cookies. The design is useful at back-to-school, teacher appreciation and end-of-year celebrations. The large yellow icing area provides a great canvas for piping a student's or teacher's name!

Yield: *7 cookies*

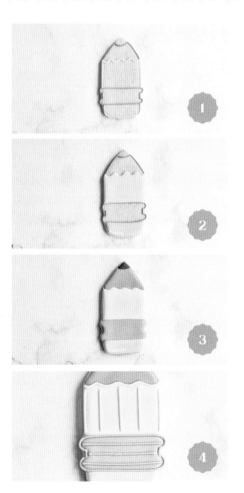

OUTLINE THE COOKIES

Step 1: Start by outlining the metal piece on the pencil using gray piping icing and a tip #2. Add the eraser outline using pink piping icing and a tip #2. Pipe the main body of the pencil using yellow piping icing and a tip #2. Add a wavy line between the yellow and brown area. Then finish the outline by piping the wood tip using light brown piping icing and a tip #2.

FLOOD THE COOKIES

Step 2: Fill in the main section of the pencil using yellow flood icing. Fill the eraser using the light pink flood icing. While the base pink icing is still wet, add a highlight to the eraser using white flood icing.

Stop and dry the iced cookies in front of a fan for 1 hour before flooding the next sections.

Step 3: Fill in the metal connector with gray flood icing. Then flood the wood tip using light brown flood icing. Add the lead tip using the black flood icing.

Stop and dry the iced cookies in front of a fan for 30 minutes before adding the details.

ADD THE DETAILS

Step 4: Pipe gray lines to add texture to the metal connector. As with the connector, pipe five yellow lines using a tip #2.

Colorful Crayon Cookie

Make the whole rainbow or keep these crayons simple with a single sky blue color. This another great cookie for personalization. Instead of the title of the color, a teacher or student name can be added. This is especially fun if using rainbow colors!

Yield: *7 cookies*

OUTLINE THE COOKIES

Step 1: Outline the crayon body and tip using the blue piping icing and a tip #2.

FLOOD THE COOKIES

Step 2: Fill in the main body of the crayon and the tip using the blue flood icing.

Stop and dry the iced cookies in front of a fan for 1 hour before flooding the next sections.

Step 3: Fill in the small section of the tip using the blue flood icing. Then pipe two small sections on the top and bottom of the crayon using black piping icing and a tip #2. Using the same black icing and tip, outline an oval in the center. Flood these three small sections using black flood icing.

Stop and dry the iced cookies in front of a fan for 30 minutes before adding the details.

ADD THE DETAILS

Step 4: Add a wiggly line on each of the small black icing areas using white piping icing and a tip #2. Add the name of the crayon color. I chose to make the blue crayon (a shorter name), spacing out the four letters of the word and using all caps.

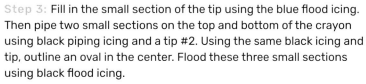

Trick or Treat

I have fond memories of trick or treating as a child. My mom knew funny pumpkin songs and we used to sing together as we walked from house to house. We collected our candy and then my brother and sister and I would spill out our buckets and trade for our favorites. We loved the neighbors that made special treat bags. Such fun memories of the sweets of the holiday formed the inspiration for this cookie collection!

The feature cookie of this platter is the Trick or Treat Pumpkin Cookie. The accent cookies are the caramel apple, candy corn and wrapped candy cookies. You can make these cookies as a set or just pick one design to keep things simple. Just keep in mind that the feature Trick or Treat Pumpkin Cookie has more steps and is the most time-consuming to create.

Yield: *21 cookies total (5 caramel apples, 5 candy corn, 6 wrapped candy and 5 pumpkins)*

TO MAKE THIS PLATTER YOU'LL NEED

- 1 batch Foolproof Cut-Out Cookie dough (page 12)
- 1 batch Royal Icing (page 14)
- Icing colors (I used Chefmaster, see "Colors by the Ounce")

CUTTERS

- Caramel Apple cookie cutter
- Rounded Pumpkin cookie cutter
- Candy Corn cookie cutter
- Wrapped Candy cookie cutter

TIPS AND TOOLS

- 5 tips #2
- 1 tip #3
- 5 couplers
- 12 icing bags (5 icing bags for piping and 7 bags, or bottles, for flooding)
- Parchment paper
- Cookie sheets
- Toothpick or scribe
- Trick or Treat stencil
- Icing scraper
- Halloween-themed sprinkles
- Coffee filter

STEP 1: PREP THE COOKIES

Use the Foolproof Cut-Out Cookie Recipe on page 12 to bake your cookies, cutting five of the caramel apple, candy corn and pumpkin, and cutting six of the wrapped candy.

STEP 2: MIX THE ICING AND PREP THE COLORS

Use the Royal Icing Recipe on page 14 to mix a single batch of icing (18 to 20 ounces [530 to 600 ml]). Divide the icing into bowls and make the seven icing colors according to the guide on the following page.

STEP 3: ADJUST THE ICING CONSISTENCY

When you're ready to decorate, adjust the consistency of the different icing colors to create stiff icing, piping icing and flooding icing, according to the amounts on the following page. For a refresher on making icing consistencies, see page 16. Once the colors are ready, prep them into piping bags, referring to the individual decorating tutorials for details.

(Continued)

Trick or Treat (Continued)

- White Icing: 3 oz (90 ml) (1 oz [30 ml] for pipe and 2 oz [60 ml] for flood)
- Black Icing: 2 oz (60 ml) (1 oz [30 ml] for *stiff* pipe and 1 oz [30 ml] for flood)
- Lemon Yellow Icing: 1 oz (30 ml) (for flood only)
- Super Red Icing: 2 oz (60 ml) (1 oz [30 ml] for pipe and 1 oz [30 ml] for flood)
- Sunset Orange Icing: 6 oz (180 ml) (for flood only)
- Purple Icing: 3 oz (90 ml) (1 oz [30 ml] for pipe and 2 oz [60 ml] for flood)
- Caramel Icing (mix equal parts Buckeye Brown and Lemon Yellow): 3 oz (90 ml) (1 oz [30 ml] for pipe and 2 oz [60 ml] for flood)

Now that your cookies and icing are prepped, it's time to decorate! Use the instructions for each individual cookie to help decorate this Trick or Treat cookie platter!

Trick or Treat Pumpkin Cookie

No tricks here! Just pumpkin treats! Don't be intimidated by this design. It looks impressive, but the stencil is going to do the hard work! Stenciling with royal icing on cookies is a great technique for adding precise text or images to your cookies. Just be sure to allow enough dry time on the base layer of icing before stenciling so you don't dent the icing.

Yield: *5 cookies*

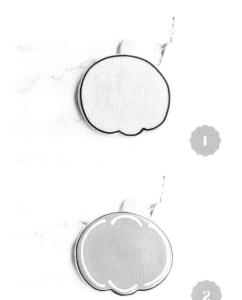

OUTLINE THE COOKIES

Step 1: Outline the pumpkin with black icing and a tip #2. When I stencil, I often like to match the colors of the cookie outline to the color of the stenciled icing. In this case, it's the black icing.

FLOOD THE COOKIES

Step 2: Generously flood the pumpkin using the orange flood icing. While the orange base is still wet, use yellow flood icing to add the pumpkin highlights. This wet-on-wet technique will allow the highlights to lay flat in the icing as a smooth base for the stenciling. Since there will be stenciled text in the center of the cookie, keep the yellow accents to the perimeter.

Stop and dry the iced cookies in front of a fan for at least 6 hours before stenciling the details. The base icing needs to set up before applying pressure on the surface. This will prevent dents and cracks. And remember, it's helpful to work in groups of cookies. While one tray is drying, move on to the next tray. See my notes on decorating in an assembly line on page 25.

ADD THE DETAILS

Stenciling Tips: Make sure to use a stiff consistency icing as described on page 17 to stencil. If the icing is too thin, it will ooze under the stencil and you won't get a clear image. The stiffer icing will hold in place, providing better results.

(Continued)

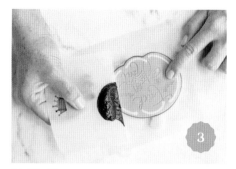

Stenciling Tips (Continued): I recommend using an icing "scraper" to evenly spread the icing on the surface of the stencil. You can find this at most online cookie supplies shops and some craft stores in the baking aisle.

Stencil multiple cookies with the same stencil and scraper. Usually, I can stencil six to twelve cookies before I need to clean the stencil. You'll know when you need to clean your stencil. The image will become less clear or sometimes the icing will build up or get on the underside of the stencil, requiring a clean before stenciling more cookies.

Cleaning the stencil is easy. Gently wipe clean with soap and warm water and rinse. Sandwich the stencil between two paper towels to thoroughly dry before using on the cookie. Any small drops of water on the stencil will dissolve the icing on the surface of the cookie, so make sure it is completely dry before using.

Stencil first before adding any other details to the cookie. You'll need the stencil to lay flat on the cookie.

Step 3: Squeeze stiff black piping icing onto your icing scraper. Center the stencil on the cookie and hold it in place with an anchor finger (or you could use a Stencil Genie or stencil frame to hold the stencil in place).

Step 4: Then, using the scraper, slide the icing across the surface of the stencil. Be generous when you spread the icing and make sure you cover all areas of the stencil. Sometimes I'll slide the icing scraper across the stencil three or four times to get it completely covered. Before you lift the stencil, use the edge of the scraper and pass over the stencil one last time to remove any excess icing. When you remove the excess, it will make reusing the stencil easier.

Step 5: Now it's time to lift and reveal the words. Gently peel back the stencil (like a sticker) and pull it away.

Step 6: Use the brown piping icing and a tip #2 to add the pumpkin stem. I squeeze the icing bag with strong hand pressure to make the stem wide at the top and then ease off to create a thinner line as I pipe it to the top of the pumpkin.

For an extra pop of color and texture, add some sprinkles at the top of the pumpkin. Pipe a line of orange icing with a tip #2 and press sprinkles into it. I used the same sprinkle mix as used on the caramel apple.

Ooey Gooey Caramel Apple Cookie

What's not to love about this classic Halloween treat? It's a little bit healthy and a little bit indulgent—but the cookie version is 100 percent indulgent! To make this cookie with a Halloween twist, we are going to add fun themed sprinkles—eyes optional!

Yield: *5 cookies*

OUTLINE THE COOKIES

Step 1: First outline the caramel section using the caramel (brown-and-yellow food color) piping icing and a tip #2. Pipe the wiggly line first, to make the caramel look like it is a drip coating on the apple. Then outline the apple using red piping icing and a tip #2. Finish the cookie outlines by piping the stick using white piping icing and a tip #2.

FLOOD THE COOKIES

Step 2: Flood the red apple section first using the red flood icing. While that red base layer of icing is still wet, add a highlight to the apple using a teardrop shape of white flood icing.

Stop and dry the iced cookies in front of a fan for 1 hour before flooding the next sections.

Step 3: Flood the stick. Creating the stripes will be a wet-on-wet pattern. Flood the white first and while that icing is still wet, add the black stripes with the black flood icing. Flood the caramel with the light brown-and-yellow flood icing. Immediately place the cookie on a coffee filter and, while the caramel icing surface is still wet, add the Halloween sprinkles. I like to pour the sprinkles in a small dish and add sprinkles by the pinch.

Stop and dry the iced cookies in front of a fan for 30 minutes before adding the details.

ADD THE DETAILS

Step 4: Pipe an accent line at the top of the apple using red icing and a tip #2. Then pipe an accent line at the top of the caramel to exaggerate the drip.

Classic Candy Corn Cookie

The candy corn cookie is one treat you can make all season long! This is a classic and is so fun to make because it doesn't require any added details. Plus, the contrast of the black outline really makes the white, orange and yellow shine!

Yield: *5 cookies*

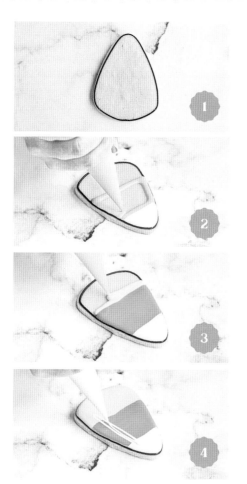

OUTLINE THE COOKIES

Step 1: Outline the candy corn cookie using black piping icing and a tip #2. The pop from the black outline is a simple detail that really impacts the look of the cookie, plus it eliminates the question of how to outline using the three colors of the flood.

FLOOD THE COOKIES

Step 2: Flooding this cookie is sort of like a wet-on-wet technique since we want the surface to be flat. First, use the white flood icing and fill in the top third section of the candy corn. Then, while the white icing is still wet, use the orange flood and fill the center. Bump the flood against the white to create a flat and smooth seam between the colors.

Step 3: Then, while the orange is still wet, flood in the bottom section with yellow. If you notice any uneven transitions between the different sections of color, add one more line of the flood icing to make the lines precise.

Step 4: While those three colors are still wet, add the white highlight using the white flood icing. If any of the icing areas are raised, shimmy the cookie to settle the icing.

Halloween Wrapped Candy Cookie

The wrapped candy cookie is the simplest cookie from this platter. I like making these purple to enhance the Halloween color palette, but you can use up your leftover icing colors. This candy would look fun in orange and yellow, too!

Yield: *6 cookies*

OUTLINE THE COOKIES

Step 1: Outline the candy cookie using purple piping icing and a tip #2.

FLOOD THE COOKIES

Step 2: Flood the entire cookie with purple flood icing.

Stop and dry the iced cookies in front of a fan for 1 hour before adding the details.

ADD THE DETAILS

Step 3: Add the swirl to the cookie. Switch your black icing bag from a tip #2 to a tip #3 to create a thicker line. Start in the center of the swirl and pipe in a circular motion moving out to the edge of the cookie. Add four wrapper lines on both ends of the cookie.

Give Thanks

Mix up the classic Thanksgiving dessert spread with a platter of beautiful, decorated cookies. The muted color palette from this set will also complement your tablescape and Thanksgiving decor!

The feature cookie of this platter is the wreath. The accent cookies are the Bumpy Pumpkin Cookies and the Speckled Leaf Cookies. You can make these cookies as a set or just pick one design to keep things simple. Just keep in mind that the feature wreath cookie has more steps and is the most time-consuming to create.

Yield: *21 cookies total (7 wreaths, 7 bumpy pumpkins and 7 speckled maple leaves)*

TO MAKE THIS PLATTER YOU'LL NEED

- 1 batch Foolproof Cut-Out Cookie dough (page 12)
- 1 batch Royal Icing (page 14)
- Icing colors (I used Chefmaster, see "Colors by the Ounce")

CUTTERS

- Wreath cookie cutter
- Rounded Pumpkin cookie cutter
- Maple Leaf cookie cutter

TIPS AND TOOLS

- 6 tips #2
- 3 tips #1
- 1 Wilton tip #67
- 6 couplers
- 12 icing bags (6 icing bags for piping and 6 bags, or bottles, for flooding)
- Square food-safe brush
- Small mixing dish
- Eyedropper
- Alcohol or a clear extract like lemon or vanilla
- Food service gloves (optional)
- Parchment paper
- Cookie sheets
- Toothpick or scribe

STEP 1: PREP THE COOKIES

Use the Foolproof Cut-Out Cookie Recipe on page 12 to bake your cookies, cutting seven of each cookie cutter design.

STEP 2: MIX THE ICING AND PREP THE COLORS

Use the Royal Icing Recipe on page 14 to mix a single batch of icing (18 to 20 ounces [530 to 600 ml]). Divide the icing into bowls and make the seven icing colors according to the guide below.

STEP 3: ADJUST THE ICING CONSISTENCY

When you're ready to decorate, adjust the consistency of the different icing colors to create piping icing and flooding icing according to the amounts below. For a refresher on making icing consistencies, see page 16. Once the colors are ready, prep them into piping bags, referring to the individual decorating tutorials for details.

COLORS BY THE OUNCE

- Ivory Icing: 4 oz (120 ml) (1 oz [30 ml] for pipe and 3 oz [90 ml] for flood)
- Dark Orange Icing (mix equal parts Sunset Orange and Ivory): 4 oz (120 ml) (1 oz [30 ml] for pipe and 3 oz [90 ml] for flood)
- Pastel Orange Icing: ½ oz (15 ml) (for flood only)
- Golden Yellow Icing: 3 oz (90 ml) (1 oz [30 ml] for pipe and 2 oz [60 ml] for flood)
- Tulip Red Icing: 3 oz (90 ml) (1 oz [30 ml] for pipe and 2 oz [60 ml] for flood)
- Avocado Green Icing: 3 oz (90 ml) (1 oz [30 ml] for pipe and 2 oz [60 ml] for flood)
- Buckeye Brown Icing: 2 oz (60 ml) (for pipe only)

Now that your cookies and icing are prepped, it's time to decorate! Use the instructions for each individual cookie to help decorate this Give Thanks cookie platter!

Give Thanks Wreath Cookie

The wreath cookie is a combination of the complete fall icing color palette. It also has interesting textures, making it the central cookie on the plate! The various details and textures of this cookie coordinate well with the simpler bumpy pumpkin and speckled leaves.

Yield: *7 cookies*

OUTLINE THE COOKIES

Step 1: First outline the ribbon section using tulip red piping icing and a tip #2. Outline each section of the ribbon to create a more dimensional bow. Outline the top wreath area using ivory piping icing and a tip #2.

FLOOD THE COOKIES

Step 2: Flood the wreath section using ivory flood icing. Flood the tails of the ribbon using tulip red flood icing.

Stop and dry the iced cookies in front of a fan for 1 hour before flooding the next section. It's helpful to work in groups of cookies. While one tray is drying, move onto the next tray. See my notes on decorating in an assembly line on page 25.

Step 3: First, flood the loops using tulip red flood icing.

Stop and quick dry the iced cookies in front of a fan for 30 minutes before flooding the next section.

Flood the center of the ribbon using tulip red flood icing. Allowing each little section of the ribbon to dry in this order creates distinct icing areas and brings the ribbon to life!

Stop and dry the iced cookies in front of a fan for 30 minutes before adding the details.

ADD THE DETAILS

Step 4: Add the vine to the side of the wreath using avocado green piping icing and the tip #1. To create the vine, first pipe the center line. Then add seven teardrops of icing on either side, pulling each drop into the center line.

Step 5: Start the wreath branches. Pipe a half circle using buckeye brown piping icing and the tip #1.

Step 6: Build up the branches. Pipe a wiggly line over the first line using brown piping icing and the tip #1.

Step 7: Add two more wiggly lines using brown piping icing and the tip #1. Four lines total looks full but still allows room for text in the center. Add dots of color to the branches using the various piping icing colors and a tip #2. Add detail lines to the ribbon using tulip red icing and a tip #2. These detail lines added to the ribbon bring that section to the foreground.

Step 8: This step is optional because the wreath looks beautiful with or without the words. But, if you want to add the text to the wreath, icing consistency is key. Make sure you are using soft-peak piping consistency, as described on page 16. This consistency is perfect for writing words. If the icing it too thick, it will be hard to pipe smooth letters. If the icing is too thin, the letters won't hold their shape.

Before piping on the cookie, I like to visually see how the words will look on the cookie. I sketch or print a sample on plain printer paper and match it up with the cutter to make sure the text fits well in the space. I have also piped directly on the paper, over the sample, to practice before jumping onto the cookie. Pay attention to spacing. Use the pumpkin orange piping icing and the tip #1 to add the text.

Bumpy Pumpkin Cookie

For this pumpkin, we are using the same rounded cookie cutter from the Trick or Treat cookie set on page 131, but we are amping it up with tons of bumpy texture.

Yield: *7 cookies*

OUTLINE THE COOKIES

Step 1: Outline the pumpkin with pumpkin orange icing and a tip #2. Outline the center section first and then pipe the sides. These are the three icing areas that will create the bumps on the pumpkin.

FLOOD THE COOKIES

Step 2: Generously flood the side areas of the pumpkin using the pumpkin orange flood icing.

Stop and dry the iced cookies in front of a fan for 1 hour before flooding the next section.

Step 3: Then flood the center of the pumpkin.

Stop and dry the iced cookies in front of a fan for 30 minutes before adding the details.

ADD THE DETAILS

Step 4: Add bumps using the pastel pumpkin orange flood icing. Vary your hand squeeze to create small, medium and large drops of icing.

Stop and dry the iced cookies in front of a fan for 30 minutes.

Add the dark orange bumps using flood icing. Then, pipe vine loops on top of the pumpkin using avocado green piping icing and a tip #2. I typically loop once in each direction. Use the brown piping icing and a tip #2 to add the pumpkin stem, starting with a strong squeeze at the top and then easing off at the bottom. Add the leaf using avocado piping icing and the tip #67. Wiggle side to side a bit as you use a strong squeeze at the base then ease off the pressure to make a thin point. See the final image at the top of the page for these details.

Speckled Leaf Cookie

Fill out the Give Thanks cookie platter with maple leaves using all your icing colors! The speckled effect is super fun—*and* super easy—to create! The photos show this technique used on a maple leaf, but it would work just as well on other leaf shapes such as oak.

Yield: *7 cookies*

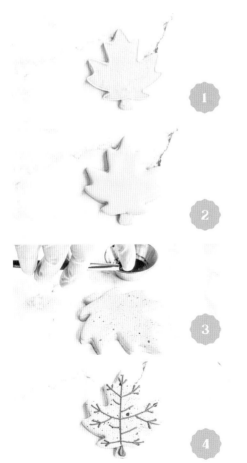

OUTLINE THE COOKIES

Step 1: Outline the leaf using golden yellow piping icing (or the color of your choice) and a tip #2.

FLOOD THE COOKIES

Step 2: Flood the entire leaf generously using the golden yellow flood icing.

Stop and dry the iced cookies in front of a fan for 1 hour before adding the details.

ADD THE DETAILS

Step 3: Add the speckles. In a small mixing bowl, add a drop of brown food gel and 3 to 4 drops of alcohol (grain or vodka work well) or extract. Mix with a square food safe brush until the gel is dissolved. I suggest wearing a glove for this step to keep your hands from getting too messy. Dip the square brush into the brown liquid. Holding the brush over the cookie, run your finger along the tip of the brush, flicking dots and splattering them onto the cookie. Repeat a few times to get an even application of speckles.

Step 4: Pipe veins on the leaf using brown piping icing and a tip #2. In the maple leaf (a pointed leaf), I piped a branch-style vein.

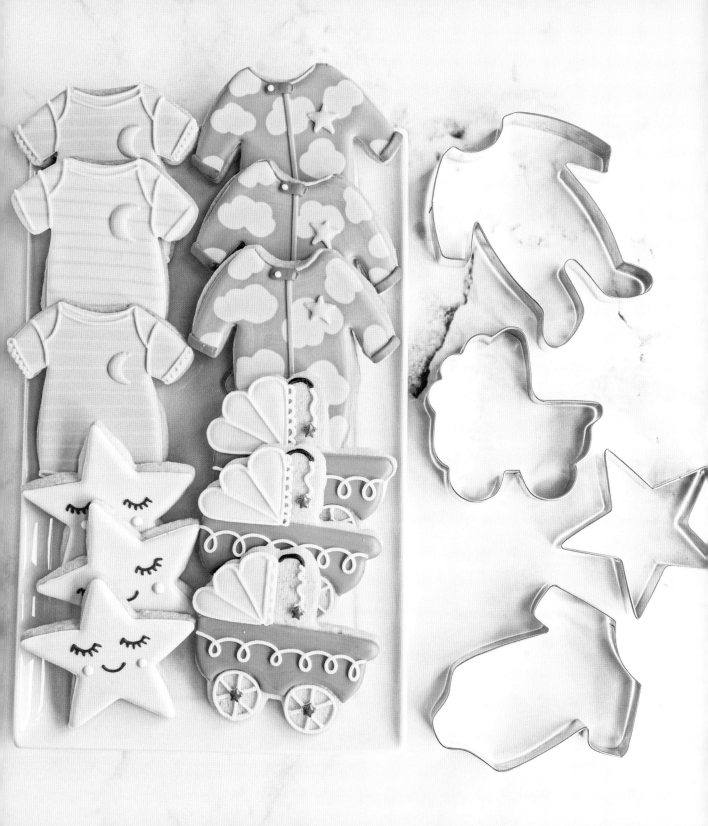

Resources

Can't get enough of cookie decorating and all things cookie? With this list you can find the supplies I use regularly and trust—including cutters, stencils, tools, food gels, sprinkles, dusts and so much more!

EQUIPMENT

The Flour Box: My online cookie supply shop, where you can find everything you need to cookie with confidence.

- www.flourbox.com
- We carry all of the cutters, stencils, tips, colors and tools featured in this book.

Ann Clark Cookie Cutters: One of my favorite brands for cutters.

- www.annclarkcookiecutters.com
- Cutters from this source are used for the Rainbow Cake (page 32), Present (page 35), Cupcake (page 34), Footie Pajama (page 38), Body Suit (page 43), Star (page 42), Carriage (page 40), Wedding Cake (page 49), Diamond Ring (page 46), Sweater (page 54), Hot Cocoa (page 56), Snowflake (page 58), Santa (page 63), Elf (page 65), Reindeer (page 67), Dove (page 73), Hot Air Balloon (page 78), Cloud (page 81), Arrow (page 80), Barn (page 84), Bunny (page 88), Chicken (page 86), Seed Packet (rectangle) (page 92), Boot (page 94), Flower (page 97), Grill (page 105), Hot Dog (page 106), Crayon (page 127), USA Map (page 110), Firecracker (page 112), Popsicle (page 113), Flip-Flop (page 116), Apple (page 124), Pumpkin (page 131), Candy Corn (page 134), Wrapped Candy (page 135), Wreath (page 138), Maple Leaf (page 141) and Oak Leaf (page 141).

Off the Beaten Path: A huge selection of affordable cutters.

- www.cookiecutter.com
- Cutters from this source are used for the Woodland Tree (page 72), Cheeseburger (page 103), Swimsuit (page 118) and Pencil (page 126).

American Traditions Cookie Cutters: A small mom-and-pop cutter shop with unique designs.

- www.americantraditioncookiecutters.com
- Cutters from this source are used for the Wedding Dress (page 48), Sun Hat (page 119) and Caramel Apple (page 133).

R & M International: A full line of cookie and baking supplies.

- www.morethanbaking.com
- Cutters from this source are used for the Watering Can (page 96) and the Egg (page 89).

The Cookie Countess: An amazing company that is known for their extensive stencil selection and more.

- www.thecookiecountess.com
- Stencils from this source are used for Trick or Treat (page 131) and Stars (page 111).

(Continued)

Chefmaster: Professional food color.

- www.chefmaster.com
- All gels and colors featured in the book are from Chefmaster.

A Note on Icing Colors: Coloring icing is essential to the cookie decorating process and therefore I choose to use gels. I prefer to use the Chefmaster brand of color. It's highly concentrated and colors the icing very well (I love the dropper top bottles). There are several other comparable gel brands like Wilton (found in craft stores) that can work as a good substitute for Chefmaster.

Creative Cookier: The inventor of the Stencil Genie and source of tools and ingredients to make baking better.

- www.creativecookier.com
- I source my Stencil Genie and meringue powder from them.

The Sugar Art: A full line of colors, dusts and edible glitters.

- www.thesugarart.com
- I like their Diamond Dust for adding edible glitter to cookies.

COOKIE PACKAGING: COOKIE BOXES, BAGS AND RIBBONS

BRP Box Shop: A great selection of cookie and bakery boxes.

- www.brpboxshop.com

Ribbon by Design: Unique ribbon and custom ribbon designs.

- www.ribbonbydesign.com

Papermart: Find boxes, tissue paper and crinkle.

- www.papermart.com

Many cutters, tools and supplies can also be found in the food crafting aisle of big box craft stores. Find oodles of cookie cutters and stencils on popular sites like etsy.com.

SHOW ME THE COOKIES!

Follow The Flour Box on social media on Instagram, Facebook, YouTube and Pinterest. Tag *@theflourboxshop* so I can see what you create!

Cookie Templates

To use a template on a cookie, follow these steps. First, copy this page or trace the template onto a piece of parchment paper. Then cut out the essential elements that need to be traced (e.g., the strap on the sandal). Be precise with your cuts to make the tracing accurate. Use a food-safe marker and trace the image to put guidelines onto the cookie. I recommend using yellow so it blends in more with the color of the cookie and won't show through the icing. Once the lines are traced on the cookie, you're ready to trace the design.

ELF FACE COOKIE
(PAGE 65)

JOLLY SANTA FACE
COOKIE (PAGE 63)

LAID-BACK LEATHER
SANDAL COOKIE (PAGE 116)

Piping Practice Sheet

Photocopy this page and slide it under a piece of parchment paper to practice these basic icing accents and techniques.

Piping Lines: Use a tip #2 and squeeze the icing bag with medium hand pressure. If you see icing pops, increase your squeeze and show that icing who's boss! Don't drag the tip on the surface, but rather touch down at the start of the line to drop an "icing anchor" and then lift up and off the sheet, allowing the icing to fall into place. With even hand pressure, lift the icing line across and touch gently down at the end.

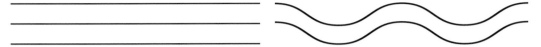

Outlining Cookies: Follow the same notes for piping lines, using a tip #2 and squeezing the icing bag with medium hand pressure. Touch down at each point for easy transitions. If you're right-handed, try piping the circle counter clockwise, and if you're left-handed try it clockwise. This will reduce blind spots!

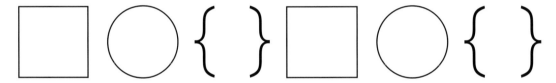

Bead Border: Use round tip #2 or star tip #13 and hold the icing bag at a 45-degree angle. Create a teardrop of icing, starting with a strong squeeze and pulling a small tail out at the end. Then overlap the next teardrop over the tail. Continue overlapping teardrops to create this beautiful accent line.

Dots: Keep the icing bag upright. Squeeze the bag and allow the icing to build up. Round off at the end with a gentle swirl to tap the tip down and prevent the "kiss" effect.

Teardrops and Hearts: Teardrops can be created with a strong squeeze and then a release on hand pressure as you pull out the tail. To make cute icing hearts, pipe two teardrops side by side so the tails overlap on the bottom.

Loops: Let your icing tip motion guide the loops. Don't rush! Take your time and avoid adding too many loops than will fit on the cookie.

Acknowledgments

Just like a cookie recipe has several essential ingredients, so does a cookie book. Just a few thoughts of thanks . . .

All my gratitude to Jesus for creating us to be creative people and using something as silly as cookie decorating as part of His plan.

Toph, Grace and Cecelia—you guys are my world. We do everything together. Thanks for being my design review team as I worked through the pages of this book. Toph, thanks for doing the dishes and the laundry so I could focus on writing. You are one of a kind and the biggest blessing in my life.

I owe everything to my original baking buddy, my mom. I wish she were here to see this book, but everything I am and do is a result of her love.

My family has walked alongside of me every step of the way. Thank you especially to my brother and sister, Andrew and Sarah, for being my biggest cheerleaders. Thank you to my dad and step-mother, Sue, who got me started with my oven and mixer. And thanks to my in-laws, Nancy and Greg, who have walked alongside Toph and me every step of this cookie journey.

Thank you to The Flour Box team: Kristyn, Stacy, Amy, Anne, Janet, Andy and Tim. Thank you for always doing everything with excellence. It's a privilege to work with each of you.

Sweet thanks to Sarah, my editor, for the valuable feedback and encouragement throughout the entire book process.

I'm beyond grateful to my talented photographer, Elise Celucci. You take beautiful photos and I'm so grateful we were able to collaborate on this project.

Sweet thanks to my BFFs from school, who were some of my first customers—Jessie, Kelly, Brandi and Staci. I couldn't love you guys more.

To the women in my life who support me as a friend, mom and business owner—Anne, Janet, Jess, Cyndie and Lynnette.

To my pastor, Jonathan, who helps me find purpose in all things, even cookies.

Sweet thanks to my cookie friends—Georganne, Hillary, Callye, Angela, Tiffany, Liz, Lisa and Stephanie! I'm so glad strangers from the Internet turned out to be really sweet people.

Many sweet thanks to the larger cookie community. I love that it is a sweet and safe space to express creativity. I love being a small crumb in the larger cookie jar.

Thanks to all The Flour Box customers! Where would I be without you? "Thank you" hardly seems sufficient!

And last, but certainly not least, sweet thanks to the entire team at Ann Clark Cookie Cutters for making the best darn cutters in the world. Ann, Ben, John and the rest of the Ann Clark team—this book would not have been possible without your help.

About the Author

Anne Yorks is the owner of The Flour Box, a cookie studio, cookie education source and online supplies shop. Anne is passionate about teaching others how to decorate and has created an extensive catalog of cookie decorating video tutorials and three in-depth online classes. Anne lives in Centre Hall, Pennsylvania, with her husband, Topher, two daughters, Grace and Cecelia, and their cat, Sprinkles!

A baker since a very young age, Anne is self-taught and has perfected her recipes and cookie techniques over years of trial and error. This passion turned into a career. Anne started decorating cookies with royal icing in 2007 when she became a stay-at-home mom and pursued her dreams of starting her own company. With the help of family and friends, she converted her two-car garage into a pink bakery and let the flour fly!

During the early years, Anne decorated thousands and thousands and thousands of cookies for big and small clients—each cookie handcrafted with love.

The demand to share decorating tips with cookie enthusiasts led to a new phase of the business. Anne no longer takes cookie orders, but still makes cookies for friends and family. The Flour Box has moved and grown into a bigger space with a cookie studio and online supplies shop. Anne loves teaching in person and through online decorating classes to help others find joy and purpose through cookies.

Got a cookie decorating story to share? You can get in touch with Anne at anne@flourbox.com. Follow The Flour Box on social media on Instagram, Facebook, YouTube and Pinterest. Tag *@theflourboxshop* so Anne can see what you create!